Setting Up and Running a Successful Small Business

Kelvin Worthington

Published by

MELROSE
BOOKS

An Imprint of Melrose Press Limited
St Thomas Place, Ely
Cambridgeshire
CB7 4GG, UK
www.melrosebooks.com

FIRST EDITION

Cover designed by Tanya Fukes

ISBN 978 1 906050 21 4

Printed and bound in Great Britain by:
CPI Antony Rowe, Bumpers Farm,
Chippenham, Wiltshire, SN14 6LH, UK

Contents

About the Author

Kelvin Worthington has over 25 years' experience in Business Banking, both in the UK and Australia. He currently runs his own business, advising clients on the setting up and running of their businesses.

During his time in the UK he was a Small Business Advisor for a major UK bank and also a volunteer Business Mentor with The Prince's Trust, a charitable organisation set up to help young people establish and run their own businesses.

Kelvin has an Honours Degree in Financial Services from the University of Central England, UK. His degree disciplines include Strategic Management, Marketing, Management of Company Finance, Accounting, Strategic Management of IT, Statistics, Decision Techniques and Quantitative Methods.

Kelvin is also an Associate of the Chartered Institute of Bankers (London).

Introduction

There is a tale told about a person who asked a wise old businessman, 'How do I go about having a small business?' The wise old businessman's reply was 'Buy a big business and wait!'

As with all good humour there is a modicum of truth in this reply. The wise old businessman recognised that people who set up their own businesses often lack the necessary skills needed to run them successfully and, hence, many of these businesses ultimately fail. In the UK it is estimated that there are over 4 million small businesses. Unfortunately many of them will not survive to see their third birthday. This is a sad but true fact.

Often people who set up their own business are very skilled at something, for example a wedding photographer is highly skilled at photography, but being skilled at one thing is only part of the story of a successful business. You will need to add more skills to your skill set if your business is to reach its full potential. These may include skills such as business planning, marketing, human resources management, finance, strategic planning and bookkeeping. It may help to think of running a business as being like a jigsaw puzzle. If one or two parts are missing then the picture is not complete and the jigsaw does not work.

The aim of this book is to provide practical, easy to understand help to people thinking of setting up their own business. It will provide guidance and improve your skills in all the areas needed for your business to be successful.

Setting up and running your own business can be a daunting prospect, but it can also bring great personal satisfaction, independence, freedom to be one's own boss, flexibility to manage the business around your lifestyle and, hopefully, financial reward. Talk to any person running their own business and some, if not all, of these motivations will emerge as the driving forces which caused that person to leave the security of a paid position with an employer and set out on the journey of establishing a successful small business.

Arguably the biggest disadvantage of running your own business is the fact that you will no longer be in receipt of a regular pay cheque each month, fortnight or week. This is probably the biggest hurdle people face when trying to decide whether or not to set up their own business. Indeed, a lot of people find this too big a hurdle for them and either decide not to set up their own business because of it, or give up running their own business and revert to working for someone else instead. This is an important issue and one which requires careful thought and planning, both from a financial and a personal perspective.

Setting up your own business involves a process of taking an idea and developing that idea into a viable business. It requires courage, vision, energy, enthusiasm and focus for an idea to evolve into a successful business. This book seeks to provide some practical help along that journey by setting out some basic steps which, if followed, will provide a firm foundation for a successful small business.

All new businesses start with an idea, or as it may sometimes be called, an opportunity. You see something which no one else has seen – perhaps a service or product which no one else is providing. That idea then grows in your mind as you think through some of the possibilities. Without realising it, you are already starting the planning process which will be absolutely vital to the success of your business. Without doubt, planning is the most important aspect of setting up and running a small business. The Business Plan will be your map and guide as you seek to develop your idea and bring it to life. To attempt to set up a small business without a business plan is a bit like visiting a foreign country for a driving holiday and not taking a map with you. You will not clearly understand where you want to go, how you are going to get there or whether you have sufficient resources to reach your destination. This would clearly be a foolhardy thing to do, and the same principle applies when setting up a small business. A Business Plan Checklist is included in the appendices to this book. The list is not exhaustive and indeed not all of the points will apply to every business in equal proportion. However, it is a framework around which you can develop a plan for your business. As you develop the plan, it will help crystallise some of the issues most vital to future success.

In setting forth on the journey of setting up and running your own business it is absolutely vital to have the support of your family. Discuss your ideas with them and make them aware of the personal and financial consequences which will come with running your own business. Obtaining their support will be absolutely vital to the success of your business. Remember also to keep them informed as the business progresses, so that they can share in the ups and downs and provide practical and emotional support as the business moves forward.

There are a number of steps which are common to all new small businesses and this book will take you through them in more detail, with the sincere hope and desire that they aid you in ensuring that your business is a long-term success.

Kelvin Worthington

1

YOUR BUSINESS IDEA

What Is Your Business Idea?

Every new business has to start somewhere and 'the idea' is always the starting point. You will have thought of a product or service which you feel you can turn into a successful business. Often, this idea is born out of a hobby or interest and this is an important aspect because if you are doing something you enjoy then you will be better at it and the chances of success multiply significantly. Remember that you intend to be running your own business for perhaps the rest of your life, or at least for a very long time, so it is important that you enjoy what you do otherwise it will become a chore and you will lose interest. If this happens the business will not reach its true potential.

The first step is to analyse what your idea is and be able to define it. For example, you may want to set up a coffee shop; or you may want to provide hairdressing services. Try to be specific in what you want to do and avoid trying to provide too many products or services, otherwise it will be difficult to focus and your business will lose direction.

Next, find out if anyone else is already offering the same product or service. If they are, think about how you can make your product or service *different* so that customers will purchase from you rather than the competition. This is called a **differentiation strategy**. The difference might be that you can offer a more personalised service; or you may be able to respond more quickly to your customers' needs because you are a smaller, more flexible business; or that your product has more features than those of your competitors. Be very careful if the only difference you can offer is price because this then becomes what is called a **low-cost strategy** and, traditionally, businesses adopting this sort of strategy are extremely vulnerable to price changes. Your competitors may be able to reduce their prices below yours and if this is the only selling point that your business has then you will be forced to reduce your prices to counter theirs. This process could go on and on until one of you finds that you cannot reduce the price any further and the business ceases. This is a very weak strategy on which to risk your whole business, so strive to provide a product or service which is intrinsically different from the competition in some way.

Vision

It is very important that you have a vision for your business. By this I mean a forward-looking 'big picture' view of your business. For example, where you want it to be in say 10 years' time. The emphasis here is on the 'big picture' rather than specific goals. The specific goals, which I will deal with later, could perhaps be called the building blocks which support the vision. They are the steps which, if successfully implemented, will enable the vision to be achieved.

The idea of having a vision for your business might seem a bit 'airy-fairy' but having a vision is vital, as it will form the overall view of what you want to achieve. Never lose sight of your vision and regularly remind yourself what the vision is.

To help you formulate the vision for your business let's look at some tools which can assist you. To begin with, try writing down some answers for yourself under the following headings, in terms of i) where you are now and ii) where you want to get to in 1, 5 and 10 years' time:

- Workload – what are your personal workload aims? Do you want to work only a certain number of hours per week in your business, or full-time?
- Location of your business – will you run your business from home, or from separate office or factory premises? You might start the business from home – but think about the future too and where you might operate from in 5 or 10 years' time.
- What will be the range of products and services that you will offer? Be specific and try to keep them to a reasonable number.
- Who will be your potential customers, and how will you reach them?
- What are your motivations for setting up and running your own business?
- How big do you want your business to grow?
- What will be your management style – autocratic, involving, inspirational, motivational? Will you, and can you, be the sort of person who leads from the front – or will you expect others to drive the business forward for you?
- What will your eventual exit strategy be – sale of the business or handover to a family member?
- What are your broad financial aims? How much will the business need to earn each year to meet all your personal financial commitments?

By honestly answering the above questions, in terms of where you are now and where you want to be, you will start to clarify the vision you have for your business.

Formulating Goals

As I have already mentioned, once you have clarified the vision, or 'big picture', you have for your business the next stage is to formulate the 'building blocks' or goals which, if achieved, will ensure that your vision is successful.

To start with, it is essential to ensure that your goals are '**SMART**' goals; that is they are:

Specific
Measurable
Achievable
Realistic
Timely

You will need to write down your goals and then review them regularly to ensure that they are still appropriate. For example, you may have achieved one goal and now need to set yourself a fresh one, or you may have discovered that a goal is no longer achievable due to a change of strategy in your business. In that case, it needs to be deleted and a fresh goal set.

There are a number of areas in which you should be setting goals for our business. These goals will be highly influenced by the original motivations which drove you to set up your business in the first place. For example, independence, a passion for your product or service, a need for better work/life balance, financial gain, or ageism in the workplace.

The areas in which you need to set goals can include:

- Financial – What level of profit do you want to make in the first year of business? Also think about what level of profit you want to be making after 5 and 10 years. You might think that trying to look that far ahead is a waste of time, but let me assure you that it is not. It is important to have longer term goals as well as shorter term ones, to help keep you focused and to help you drive your business forward.

- Marketing – How many customers do you want to have? What level of annual sales do you want to achieve? How many products or services do you want to have and how many of each product or service do you want to sell each year?
- Operations – Will you need to employ staff and if so, how many? As your business grows, will you need to employ additional staff, or will you consider out-sourcing some of the day-to-day work to contractors? What size of premises do you want and where will they be located? What equipment do you want or need to have in order to get your business started?
- Personal - What level of salary do you want to be able to take out of your business? What sort of car do you want to drive? What other personal possessions do you want to have? How much time do you want to spend with your family?

Remember that with all of the above it is important to make the goals 'SMART'. For example, when formulating a goal for what level of annual sales you want to have, ensure you put down not only the pound figure but also the date by which you want to achieve it. Be realistic in your expectations and don't set the timeframe too far out. For example, don't set yourself a goal of annual sales of £1 million in 10 years' time. Instead perhaps set yourself a goal of annual sales of £200,000 in 3 years time. Set yourself smaller, manageable goals and you will find that these will build into that bigger picture you set yourself when deciding on the vision for your business.

It is absolutely vital that you monitor the goals that you set for your business. There is absolutely no point in setting goals and then not measuring them, because you will never know if you ever actually achieve them!

Also, try to start each day by reading your business goals. This will keep you focused on the things which are important for success.

Why not write down your business goals and stick them on the wall near to where you will be working from most of the time. In this way you will see your goals every day and this will help to keep you focused on what you want to achieve in your business.

Personal Skills

When deciding to set up and run your own business it is important to be honest with yourself about the skills you have and those where you may need further help in order to bring the level up to that needed to run a business.

In all probability, you will already have experience of the line of business you intend to start. For example, photography might have been a long time hobby of yours and you have now decided to set up your own photography business. However, running a successful business requires you to have other skills as well as just the core activity. For example you will need to have:

- Communication skills – to communicate effectively with staff, customers and suppliers
- Organisational ability – to organise your own time and that of any staff you employ
- Financial skills – to manage the finances of your business
- Negotiation skills – to negotiate effectively with staff, customers and suppliers
- In addition to these more 'technical' skills you will need to have drive, determination, energy and vision.

Before embarking on running your own business it is important to carry out a self assessment of your abilities in all of the above areas. You might find it useful to score yourself out of 10 in each area. In this way you will be able to prioritise those areas where you need most help.

Once you have done this exercise, consider your weaker areas and think about how you might improve your skills in those areas. This might involve attending courses such as those run by Local Colleges, or business help organisations such as The Prince's Trust, BusinessLink and Chambers of Commerce (website addresses in the Useful Addresses section at the end of this book). Also have a look in your local library or bookshop – often they will have a separate section of books on business issues and these can help you with both general business advice and specific areas of business, for example marketing.

If you feel you cannot adequately address all of the areas in which you need to improve your skills, and you do not want to take on a business partner or employ staff to fulfil these roles for you, you could consider outsourcing the role. For example, if you have limited finance skills and do not want to employ a full or part-time finance person you might consider outsourcing the role to another person who runs a bookkeeping business, or approaching your accountant for help.

The advantage of doing this is that you obtain the skills your business needs but you do not increase the costs of your business excessively, because you will only pay for the person when you need them, rather than employing them in your business on a permanent basis.

Marketing

Once you have a clear idea of your vision and your goals, and are happy that you have the necessary skills to set up and run your business, it is important to think about how you will market your product or service.

Marketing is based on the concept that **the customer is the most important person to a business**. This is a good thing to remember, because if you don't have any customers, you don't have a business! Therefore it is all about creating a product or service which **customers will want**, at the **right price**, delivered to them in the **right way**, at an **acceptable profit** to your business.

Traditional marketing thinking is based around the concept of what is called the 'four P's'. These are:

- Product
  - Product or service range, breadth and mix.
  - Product or service features and benefits
  - Product quality
  - Packaging
- Price
  - Price levels
  - Price strategies
  - Credit policies, i.e. how long will you give your customers to pay you
- Promotion
  - Advertising, i.e. how much will you spend; what form of advertising will you use; when will you advertise, e.g. morning, evening, throughout the day
  - Publicity
  - Sales promotion, e.g. special offers
- Place
  - Distribution channels
  - Stock levels
  - Delivery

Together, the above areas form what is called the marketing mix and will comprise the basis of the marketing aspects of your business. Think of them as ingredients in a cake. To achieve a successful cake the ingredients may be required in differing quantities, but all are necessary to achieve a successful outcome. It is important therefore that you give a lot of thought to all of the above areas, as part of your marketing 'plan'. As a small business it isn't absolutely necessary to have a formal written marketing plan but you may find it helpful to at least have some brief notes so that you can refer back to them from time to time for clarification.

Also, as you develop your marketing plan you may need to go back and revise your vision and goals, because something you originally thought would be achievable may not now seem so. Therefore it is important to be flexible and to revise your original vision or goals if necessary.

Market Research

It is really important that you ask yourself if there is a market for your idea. You might think you have a great idea but will everyone else think it is a great idea too?

To help you understand if there is a viable market for your idea you should consider carrying out some market research by asking people if they would purchase your product or service, were it to become available. Carry out as much research as possible and if you receive favourable responses then you will be reassured that the idea is a good one. It may be that during your research it becomes apparent that you need to modify your idea to make it more marketable. Take notice of this feedback and be adaptable in your thinking. This will enable you to change in line with market conditions, which is a vital aspect of any business – the awareness of what is happening in the marketplace and the ability to adapt accordingly. This issue is common to all types of businesses, be they a major bank or the little corner store.

Essentially there are two options available to businesses in obtaining market research data:

1. Internal market research
2. External market research

Internal Market Research

Internal market research would normally mean either using the business's own staff to 'test' new products or services, or having an internal market research team within the business who carry out the market research on behalf of that business. Clearly, however, small businesses may not have a large number of staff, or cannot afford to have a large team of people carrying out market research. Therefore in the context of a small business, internal research might mean talking to family and trusted friends, or you personally carrying out some research by post or telephone. You may even consider carrying out some face to face research in what are called 'focus groups'. This is where you gather together a group of invited people, ask them questions about your proposed product or service, and take note of their answers to help you better formulate what products or services will be of interest to your potential customers.

The main advantage of carrying out market research yourself is that you can control the research process and adapt it as you go along, to accommodate changing circumstances. For example, you might find that the response rate to a postal research campaign is poor; in that case, you can quickly decide to drop that form of research and try something else instead.

Another key advantage of carrying out the research yourself is that by personally interviewing people you gain a much deeper understanding of their responses, because you can observe them as well as hear them. Body language is an important part of people's responses because they might say 'yes' but their body language might indicate a weak 'yes' rather than a strong 'yes'.

Additionally, if you are doing the interviewing personally you are able to take the questioning off in a different direction, if you feel it is appropriate, to gain a clearer understanding of what people are telling you. Also, you have greater flexibility to change the direction of your questioning completely if you feel that the interviewing is not going as you would like it to and you want to explore other areas.

To start with, draw up a questionnaire setting out the questions you need to know the answers to, which will help you in determining whether your product or service is one which customers will want to buy. Try to be as specific as possible in the questions, otherwise you are likely to end up with widely differing answers which will not be of much use to you. Also, try to keep the questions to a reasonable number, otherwise people will get bored answering them and may start to just answer quickly, without really thinking about their responses. Test out the questionnaire on family or trusted friends first and refine it based on their responses, so that when you launch into your full market research you will be maximising your time in the most effective way.

External Market Research

External market research in the context of a small business usually means two things:

- You can employ an external market research agency to carry out market research for you.
- You can make use of data from publicly-available sources.

Employing an external market research agency can have a number of advantages. Firstly, it gives you access to trained market research people who are able to help you in the formulation of the sorts of questions you should be asking in your questionnaire. They can also provide advice on the most cost effective strategies which you can employ to collect the research data you need.

Secondly, agencies are often able to access a much wider population than you could ever hope to. This gives you a much larger data sample, which will give you better results in terms of more opinions to work with. In turn this will enable you to better focus your product or service in areas which will bring you the greatest opportunity for success. You can find the names and addresses for market research agencies in your area by looking in Yellow Pages. Alternatively try searching the internet, but remember to refine the search criteria to your local area otherwise you may end up with the names of agencies from all around the world!

Employing an external research agency also has potential disadvantages. The first is cost, although agencies often have different levels of support they can offer. Talk to them about which 'package' might suit you best in terms of quality research at a reasonable cost.

The second disadvantage is that, to a certain extent, you lose some measure of control over the responses you are seeking to your questions. By this I mean that, as noted earlier under internal market research, if you are personally interviewing people you gain a much deeper understanding of their responses. Also, if you are doing the interviewing personally you are able to take the questioning off in a different direction if you feel it is appropriate. External research agencies will often simply collect the responses to the specific questions you want them to ask.

The other aspect of external market research, as noted earlier, is making use of data from publicly-available sources. The Office for National Statistics (website address in the Useful Addresses section at the end of this book) has a huge range of data which can help you in your market research, such as data on the economy, people, regions and the environment. The data is free. If you do not have internet access try your local library as they often carry copies of Government statistics.

Distribution

It is important to decide how you will distribute your product or service to your prospective customers. Will you deal directly with your customers, or will you need intermediaries who will act as the 'middle man' in the transaction?

A vital aspect of distribution is deciding where your business will operate from. You may decide to operate it from home or you may decide that you need an office, factory or shop.

Location is very important when choosing a business property. For example, if you plan to open a coffee shop then you will want it to be where there are lots of people passing by, so that they can see you are there and that you want to sell them coffee. It would be pointless having your coffee shop in an area where there are few people because you immediately limit your potential market. Conversely, do not take on the expense of a shop in a main street if you do not need to. Rents for main street premises are often more expensive than streets away from the main street, so consider the costs versus the benefits of where you will locate your business and do not commit to a location which is very expensive unless there is a real benefit to being in that location.

If you intend to manufacture something then try to locate as near to your suppliers and customers as possible, to cut down on delivery time and costs. For example, there would be little point manufacturing deckchairs out in the country when the majority of your potential customers are located on or near the coast. The extra time and cost of getting your product to them could make your business not viable.

Whatever type of business you are running, remember that as it grows you may need to consider moving your business from its current location to larger premises, or you may even consider purchasing business premises. Before you do this it is vital that you revisit your budget (see Chapter 2) to ensure that your business will generate sufficient profit to fund the increased costs of rent or loan repayments. Don't commit yourself to a lease or purchase of new or larger business premises without first ensuring that you have the necessary capital or finance to pay for them.

Location is less important if, for example, you want to set up an internet-based business where you never actually meet your customers face to face. Clearly this type of business can be operated from virtually anywhere, so long as the necessary information technology and communications systems are available. Of course, you don't just have to be an internet-based business to have a business website. You can use a website as a tool for attracting new customers, or for informing customers about what you are selling. You can also use your website to inform customers about the vision you have for your business, your customer service ethics, and to enable customers to purchase your goods or services online. Let's have a look at some of the issues concerning websites and Information Technology generally, in more detail.

Business Website

As mentioned earlier, you may decide to establish a website for your business. This might be simply to inform prospective customers about your product or service, or you may also use your website as the means to actually receive orders for whatever it is you are selling.

The important thing to remember with a website is that you want it to look good. One of the biggest hurdles facing a small business is portraying to the outside world that it is a professional and credible business. Having a good website can go a long way to helping you overcome this challenge.

There are numerous companies which provide what are called 'web-hosting services'. This means that they will host your website for you and ensure that it is always available to anyone who wants to visit it. They can also help you find a 'domain name' for your website. For example, if you were running an interior design business called 'City Interior Designs', it is likely that you would want your domain name to be something like

www.cityinteriordesigns.com or
www.cityinteriordesigns.co.uk

(the 'uk' bit on the end means that it is a UK domain name only, rather than a global domain name). Assuming the domain name you want is not already owned by someone else, you can purchase it through the web-hosting company and they will maintain the site for you, subject to an annual fee.

A web-hosting company can also help you with the design and functionality of your website. Often they have a number of packages available that are reasonably priced and easy to use, so that you can choose to build your own site or have them build it for you. The packages range from a simple page or couple of pages of information, to full functionality including links to other sites and provision of the ability for your customers to purchase goods from you online, via a secure payment facility.

If you are already familiar with the internet you may have used what is called a 'search engine' to find something on the world wide web. Examples of search engines include Google, MSN, Yahoo!, and Ask Jeeves. It follows therefore that for people to find your website they will probably use a search engine. Search engine companies offer packages to move your website further up their list, so that when someone carries out a search your business is listed in the first few names that appear. This obviously means that the person making the search will quickly see your business in the list and hopefully go to your website. Your web-hosting company can advise you on which would be the best solution for your business, in terms of cost and helping people find your website.

To find a list of companies which can help you with all of the above website issues, use one of the search engines, or have a look in Yellow Pages. Compare prices and packages before deciding which one to go with.

Information Technology

Most small businesses will benefit from utilising some form of information technology (IT). It will often be the way in which you communicate with the majority of your customers and suppliers, for example receiving and placing orders, as well as being vital for maintaining the essential records a business must keep. Additionally, IT can be used as the main place where you store and manage information about your customers, and a means by which you will be able to research what is happening in your market-place and what your competitors are doing.

Remember that if you are storing information on your computer about your customers you must be aware of the provisions of the Data Protection Act. This Act was passed to set the standards that organisations are required to meet in collecting, storing, using, disclosing, protecting and transferring personal information. For more information on the Data Protection Act and the requirements you will need to adhere to, have a look at the Information Commissioner's Office website (address in the Useful Addresses section at the end of this book).

At one time the idea of having a computer was thought to be beyond most people. Often the cost of equipment was prohibitive and the early computers were either too large or those that were small enough didn't have enough computing power to do all the things you need to be able to do if you are running a business. Thankfully, things have changed and it is now possible to obtain powerful computing equipment at a very affordable price. As a starting point for a small business you should aim to have as a minimum:

- A personal computer
- A printer
- A fax machine (ideally incorporating an answering machine)
- A photocopier

Office supplies stores and specialist computer stores can advise you on what sort of computer will best suit your needs, but it is still a good idea to carry out some research before purchasing one. Talk to friends who have computers and find out what speed their processor is, how much memory their computer has, and what software they are running. Also, have a look at what accounting software package you intend to use and see what the minimum requirements are (i.e. what type of computer and operating system are needed) for that package to run effectively. Armed with this sort of information you will be in a much better position to decide what sort of computer to buy.

It is also important to have systems in place for managing your IT. By this I mean, for example, what happens if your computer breaks down and all of your files stored on it are lost? Ensure that you have a policy of backing up your important files to a CD or separate hard drive storage device on a regular basis. Ideally these backup files should be stored away from your business premises in case of fire or burglary. If this is not possible, at least try to store them in a lockable, fire-proof cabinet. It is also important to be prepared for any of your IT equipment to fail, by having the necessary support in place. In the case of a small business this will often be an external computer repair person, who you can call in if your equipment fails.

Another aspect of managing your IT is protecting it from computer viruses and computer hackers (people who break into your computer over the internet and steal or corrupt your information). There are a number of software packages available which can protect you from such attacks and it is strongly advised that you install such protection on your computer. The shop where you are purchasing your computer should be able to give you some guidance on what you need and the different products available.

For efficient use of your IT, and the efficient operation of your business, you will need to have an internet connection so that you can send and receive emails and orders via your computer. What sort of connection you have will be determined by how much information you intend to communicate via the internet. If you think you will be communicating large files and lots of information then a Broadband connection might be the best way to proceed, as this gives faster response times. If you think that you will only be communicating smaller amounts of information then a simple Dial-up connection might be sufficient. Dial-up is slower than Broadband, but is often less expensive. Some areas may not have Broadband connectivity available, so you may be forced to go with Dial-up initially or alternatively you might consider what is called a Wireless connection, where the connection is via a mobile phone signal rather than down a telephone line. Again, explore the various options available before making a purchase.

Advertising

An important element of deciding how you will promote your product or service will be advertising. If you will be dealing directly with your customers you will need to think about how you will make them aware that you have a product or service which they may want to purchase. This may, for example, involve direct advertising in newspapers or periodicals, or even radio or television adverts. Another way of advertising direct to your potential customers is through your business website, as discussed earlier in this book. However, do not undertake the expense of having a website unless you feel it will bring a return for your business, by way of new customers. You may also think about using postal marketing as a way of making people aware of your product or service.

A further way of advertising might be through face to face contact. By this I mean joining organisations such as Chambers of Commerce and Business Clubs, mingling with other members there and handing out your business cards. This can be a powerful form of advertising because people get to meet you in person and if they like you they are more likely to make use of your products or services. A useful tip is to have your business cards printed with your business name and contact details on the front of the card and brief details of the products or services you are offering on the reverse. Not only will this maximise your spend on business cards but it will be useful for people you hand your card to, to help them remember what it is you are offering.

Let's have a closer look at the different types of advertising you might use, together with their respective advantages and disadvantages. Remember that you do not have to stick with just one form of advertising – you can mix the different forms as you feel appropriate. The important thing is that your overall advertising is effective.

Newspapers and Periodicals

Advertising in newspapers or periodicals can be an effective way of reaching a large number of people, relatively inexpensively. You may decide simply to take out an advert in a newspaper or periodical, or you might incorporate an advert into a news story of some sort. For example, this might be a story in your local newspaper about what you are doing; although bear in mind that you will need the story to have an 'angle' of some description otherwise the newspaper is unlikely to want to run with it.

If you decide to go down the periodical route, again you might just take out an advert or, alternatively, you might write an article for the periodical and include an advert in the article, making the readers aware of your product or service. For example, if your service is providing interior decorating advice you might write an article for an interior decorating periodical about the latest trends in colour schemes and include details of your business. In this way you will not only show people what you do, but as the periodical in question is an interior decorating magazine it is likely to be read by people considering having some interior decorating done in their home. Therefore, you will be targeting your marketing to the specific customers you want to reach.

The key questions to ask yourself before undertaking newspaper or periodical advertising are:

- What is the distribution size of the newspaper or periodical, that is, how many people purchase it?
- What age group is the newspaper or periodical aimed at? For example, there would be no point advertising zimmer frames in a teenager's magazine!
- What is the geographical spread of the newspaper or periodical? For example, does it just cover the local area, or is it regional or national in its distribution?
- What is the target market of the newspaper or periodical? Remember the interior decorating example used earlier – there would be little point writing an interior decorating article and then trying to put it in a periodical aimed at the accounting profession!

Ensure that your newspaper or periodical marketing is, as with all forms of marketing, appropriately targeted at the right audience, so that you maximise your return in terms of attracting new customers.

Radio

Advertising via the radio can be a very effective way of reaching a huge number of people. Obviously it is likely to cost more than advertising in newspapers or periodicals but it does have some significant advantages.

Radio advertising is likely to enable you to reach a greater number of people than newspaper or periodical advertising. Just consider the geographical range which radio stations have and the number of people living within that range. Of course not everyone will be listening to the same radio station but you will see that the potential number of people you can reach with your advertising message is huge.

Radio advertising also has some subliminal qualities which you do not obtain with newspaper and periodical advertising. By this I mean that if people hear the same message over and over again, over a period of time, the message gets 'stored' in their memories and will surface in response to certain stimuli. For example, if you are offering a webpage design service and you carry out a campaign of advertising over the radio it is likely that the name of your business, or the 'jingle' used in the advert, will store itself in the memories of the listeners. Then, when they think about having a web page designed for themselves, your name or jingle will pop up in their minds and they will seek you out. This might sound a bit of an odd theory but believe me, it does work!

The main disadvantage of radio advertising is that of cost. To be really effective, radio advertising needs to be repeated time and time again, and ideally have some form of catch-phrase or jingle in it. The radio station companies will help you design a catch-phrase or jingle and put all of this together into an advert, but obviously that will cost money, as will the need for repeated slots on the station.

Another disadvantage is that the message you get over to the listeners in radio advertising needs to be a simple one. The format does not lend itself to complex advertising with long product lists or trying to explain complex concepts.

The key questions to ask yourself before undertaking radio advertising are:

- What is the distribution of the radio station, that is, how many people listen to it? The radio station should be able to provide you with this information.
- What age group is the radio station aimed at? For example there would be little point in advertising skateboards on a radio station aimed at the over 65's!
- What type of listeners is the radio station trying to attract? For example, if your product or service is related to antique furniture it might be advantageous to approach a radio station which plays classical music, as these listeners are more likely to be people with an interest in antiques and have spare funds to invest.

Television

Television advertising can be an extremely effective way of promoting your product or service. The number of people you can reach via this form of advertising can be huge (consider that some television programmes have viewing numbers in the millions!) and this is one of the main advantages of television advertising.

Another advantage is that you are better able to get across a relatively complex message more easily using television advertising than is possible with, for example, radio advertising because you can use pictures as well as sound to communicate the message.

This leads to another key advantage of television advertising. It is a widely-known fact that people absorb communications which they can **see** more effectively than communications which they can only **hear**. Therefore, a television advert can have a greater impact than, for example, a radio advert.

The main disadvantage of television advertising is cost. To create a television advert you will need to have actors, a director and a team of people actually producing the advert. The television company will be able to help you with this, but it all costs money. Additionally, different time slots on television have different costs. For example, an advertising slot in the middle of a prime-time programme will cost significantly more than an advertising slot in the middle of a non prime-time programme.

The key is to weigh up the costs of television advertising against the benefits you hope to gain, which can be significant in terms of the number of people you reach and the effectiveness of the message you are trying to communicate.

As with radio advertising, ensure that your advertisement is going out at the most effective time for the target market you are aiming at. For example, you will have noticed that toy manufacturers tend to advertise heavily during children's programmes. This is not a coincidence!

Postal Marketing

Another form of advertising, and one which carries relatively low costs so is more suited to a small business, is postal marketing (sometimes called 'junk mail'). By this I mean that you obtain a list of potential customers from a direct marketing company and send those potential customers details of your product or service in the post.

However, if the person or organisation you're targeting asks to be taken off your mailing list, you must comply with their request. There are no exceptions to this rule, and if you fail to comply, they can apply to the courts for an order against you under the Data Protection Act.

The Mailing Preference Service (MPS) is a service set up by the direct marketing industry to help people who don't want to receive 'junk mail'. People simply register their details to prevent further mailings and there are codes of practice in place which specify that marketers should 'clean' their lists against the MPS file before embarking on a postal marketing campaign. In other words, you need to check that you are not going to send one of your information leaflets to someone who has expressly requested that they are not sent such things in the post.

For more targeted advertising you could draw up a list of potential customers yourself by trawling through publications such as Yellow Pages to find businesses which might use, or be interested in using, your product or service. For example, if you were selling car wash supplies you might make a list of all the car wash operators in your area and contact them.

An alternative to preparing a target list yourself is to purchase a targeted mailing list from an external supplier. Have a look in Yellow Pages for suppliers or try searching on the internet. Once you have found a supplier, talk to them about your target market and obtain an appropriately targeted list. For example, if you are providing IT support services to small and micro businesses ensure that the list contains names of businesses with fewer than say 5 employees.

Remember that it is important to monitor the effectiveness of your advertising, so that you maximise the return on your advertising investment. Also, by monitoring the responses to your advertising you can change your advertising strategy if one particular form is not working for you. For example, if you place an advert in a newspaper and get no responses whatsoever, there is little point in continuing the advert – try something different instead and see how successful that is for you.

Weigh up the costs versus the benefits of all types of advertising, because there is little point in having the expense of a particular form of advertising if it does not bring you any new customers. Monitor the response rate from each form of advertising you undertake, to find out which is the most effective, and then target your effort in that area.

Also remember that your advertising has to be fair and reasonable, and must meet the guidelines set out in legislation such as the Control of Misleading Advertisements Regulations 1988. For example, you are not permitted to promise something to a customer if you cannot deliver on that promise. Also, if there are potential downsides to your product or service then you must make potential customers aware of this. For example, if you are selling an investment which may fall in value as well as rise, then you must state this in your advertising. There is lots of useful information on the guidelines and rules covering business advertising to be found on the Office of Fair Trading website (address in the Useful Addresses section at the end of this book).

Purchasing an Existing Business

As an alternative to setting up your own business you may decide to purchase an existing business. If you do, always ensure that you obtain a minimum of the last 3 years trading results from the existing owners, preferably confirmed by their accountant. These will show you how the business has been trading and will also show any trends (good or bad) in the business. Beware if, for example, the sales have been declining in recent years. This may indicate that the product or service being provided by the business is becoming obsolete. On the other hand, declining sales may be as a result of the existing owner's lack of interest through, for example, ill health. If this is the case, it need not necessarily be a negative thing and may be an opportunity to acquire a sound underlying business. Obtain a thorough history of the business and its owners, including credit checks on the owners and/or company and ensure that you understand the breakdown of the purchase price being sought. For example, are you buying stock, goodwill, patents or a combination of these? If in doubt as to their value, consult an accountant to ensure that you do not over-pay for the business. It is vital to understand the reasons behind the present owner's desire to sell the business, and always remember that if something sounds too good to be true, then it probably is!

Purchasing a Franchise

Another option when setting up your own business is to purchase a franchise. A franchise is where you as the franchisee are granted the right to use the franchisor's name and systems. For example, McDonald's restaurants are franchises. McDonald's Corporation is the franchisor with the owner of the local McDonald's outlet being the franchisee. In return for this right to use its name and systems the franchisor is usually paid an initial sum plus a royalty, which is a percentage of the annual sales of the business.

The advantages of a franchise are that the franchisor usually supplies marketing, training and operational support to the franchisee plus, of course, an established brand name which customers will already be aware of. This helps those people starting a business who have little or no knowledge of running one and thus reduces the risk of the business failing.

The disadvantage of a franchise is that to a certain degree the business is still not your own. You are not completely free to run it as you want and have to operate it within guidelines set out by the franchisor. Additionally, it can be more costly than establishing your own business because of the initial franchise fee and subsequent royalties which have to be paid to the franchisor.

The terms of the arrangement between the two parties (franchisor and franchisee) are set out in a Franchise Agreement. You should have the agreement checked out by your solicitor before entering into it. If you do decide to buy a franchise, ensure that the product or service being supplied is something you are genuinely interested in, for the reasons outlined earlier. For example, it is no good purchasing a photographic franchise if you don't have a genuine interest in or knowledge of photography. Your customers will soon pick up on this and will be less inclined to buy from you. For more information on franchising, contact The British Franchise Association (website address in the Useful Addresses section at the end of this book).

Whichever option you decide to take – setting up your own business, buying an existing business or buying a franchise – the guidelines contained in this book still apply. They are issues which still have to be thought through and addressed if your business is to be a success.

2

Completing a Feasibility Study

Once you have decided what your product or service will be, and how you will market it to your customers, you need to work out if the idea is financially feasible. To do this you will need to work out what price you can sell your product or service for, how much of it you can sell each year and what the costs of running the business will be. This is sometimes called **preparing a budget**.

Price

You should consider selling your product or service for the maximum amount possible, after having considered what your competitors sell theirs for and what customers will pay. Again, market research will be the key in determining the maximum price you can charge. Ask people what they would be prepared to pay for your product or service and listen to their responses. Also, find out what your competitors charge and decide if you will charge a similar amount, or whether your product or service is sufficiently different that your customers would be prepared to pay a premium in purchasing from you rather than from your competitors.

Volume

The next step is to consider how much of your product or service you can sell in a year. A timeframe of a year is a good starting place when preparing a budget because some of the expenses you will incur such as electricity and telephone will generally be payable quarterly and other expenses will be monthly, so it is easier at this stage to multiply everything out to a common 12-month period. You can always, and in fact will need to, prepare a monthly budget once you have completed the annual budget. A specimen annual budget is included in the appendices to this book. Try to be realistic when considering how much of your product or service you can sell. It is better to be slightly conservative so that you build in a contingency if things don't go quite to plan. You can still set yourself a 'go for' target as well, to provide a stretching goal for yourself, but for budgeting purposes it is best to be slightly conservative.

Costs of Running the Business

Once you have calculated how much of your product or service you can sell in a year, take away what you consider to be the costs of running the business, sometimes called expenses or expenditure, in a year and whatever is left over is your profit (or loss, as the case may be).

Importantly, when preparing the budget do not forget to include a salary for yourself, at whatever level you need to meet your personal expenses such as home loan payments, council taxes, food and general living expenses. Remember that the figure to put in your budget for your salary will be before tax; so you need to 'gross up' the figure you have arrived at for your personal expenses by your expected marginal rate of tax, to arrive at the pre-tax figure. For example, if you need to receive £30,000 per annum after tax, and your marginal rate of tax is 25% then you need to put a figure of £40,000 in your budget, because after you have paid tax at the rate of 25% on £40,000 you are left with £30,000.

Profit

If, after preparing the budget, you end up with a profit, think about how big that profit is. If it is only small, then any minor change in your income or your expenditure could wipe out that profit and turn it into a loss. Think of ways in which you may be able to increase the volumes you can sell, or the price you can sell for, or ways of decreasing your expenditure so that the profit figure is as big as you can make it. This will provide you with a good 'feel' for the level of risk you are taking on. The lower the profit the higher the risk and, conversely, the higher the profit the lower the risk.

If, after completing your budget, you end up with a loss, then you need to seriously rethink your idea and look for ways to turn that loss into a profit. For example, you may be able to run your business from home rather than renting an office, thereby saving a lot of expenditure on rent and thus having your budget show a profit rather than a loss. Be realistic in your budget and if possible over-estimate your expenditure and under-estimate your income a little so that you have a contingency built in should things not quite run in line with the budget.

3

Financing Your Business

Once you have established, through the use of the feasibility study (Chapter 2), that your business is viable you then need to think about how you will finance your new business. This is an area often overlooked, or given scant attention, by people setting up their own business; but it is arguably one of the most vital elements in setting up and running a new business.

General Guidance

You need to think about the amount of capital you will need just to set the business up and also the amount you will need to keep it running. I will call the amount of capital required to set the business up the **establishment capital** and the amount required to keep it running the **working capital**. You then need to consider where this capital will come from: for example, savings, redundancy payment, borrowing from family or a bank. One word of warning here – wherever possible do not borrow money in the first two years after setting up your business. The reason for this is that the business will have enough cashflow pressures to work through without taking on the additional pressure of meeting loan repayments. Banks will not allow you to miss loan repayments and the need to meet those repayments could seriously jeopardise the future of your business. Borrowing from family is slightly better in that, generally, family will allow you greater flexibility in making repayments if you do not have the cash to make them at the required time. However, generally, the recommendation is that you do not borrow money in the first two years of operation.

If you find that you absolutely need some funding to get your business up and running, one option you might consider is The Prince's Trust. The Trust provides low interest loans and grants to people aged 18-30 who are currently unemployed. If you meet this criterion then I would recommend approaching the Trust first, rather than a bank, as its interest rates are generally lower and it tends to be more flexible if a business finds that it cannot make a repayment on its loan due to lack of cashflow. You can find more details about The Prince's Trust by visiting its website (address in the Useful Addresses section at the end of this book).

Another source of finance to explore is grants. There are a number of schemes run by central and local government, and also some private organisations. These schemes have varying qualifying criteria – such as the number of new jobs being created – so the easiest way to see if you may be eligible for any grants is to contact your local BusinessLink office. You can find the telephone number in your local telephone directory, or alternatively find your nearest office by searching on the BusinessLink website (address in the Useful Addresses section at the end of this book).

If you do decide to borrow money from a bank it is highly unlikely that you will obtain a reasonably sized loan without providing security of some sort, usually a mortgage on your home. **You need to give very careful thought before taking this step** because if the business ultimately fails the bank has the right to repossess your home and sell it to repay the loan. Your spouse or partner will need to enter into the mortgage agreement and it is absolutely vital that you are both aware of the possible consequences of taking this step. One advantage, however, of using your home as security is that your loan will be at a much reduced interest rate compared to an unsecured loan. Before you decide to put up your property as security you should seek the advice of your solicitor as to what you may be getting yourself into. In fact, most banks now insist that you do this anyway because they recognise the seriousness of the issue.

If you decide to borrow money to finance your business there are a couple of simple guidelines to follow, to ensure that you get the right sort of finance. If you are borrowing to cover timing differences caused by you having to pay for business expenses whilst waiting for your customers to pay you, then an overdraft is the best form of borrowing to have as it gives the freedom for the balance of your account to fluctuate within an agreed limit, thereby ensuring that you only pay interest on the amount you are borrowing at any one time. Interest is usually calculated daily on the balance of the account on that day. So, for example, if the balance is £1,000 overdrawn one day, then the next day you receive funds from one of your customers and the account balance changes to £500 overdrawn, you will pay one day's interest on £1,000 and one day's interest on £500. If you are borrowing money to pay for more long-term assets for your business, such as machinery or motor vehicles, then a loan is the best way to proceed as it will enable you to spread the repayments over a longer period. This means that you do not then tie up in long-term assets valuable cash which might be needed to fund the day-to-day running expenses of the business.

Establishment Capital

This is the amount of money you will need just to get your business established. It will include the cost of any machinery or equipment you will need. The following list details just some of the items which might be included in this category:

- Registration of your company (if you decide to trade as a company)
- Computer
- Telephone
- Mobile telephone
- Fax machine
- Car or van
- Desk and chair
- Insurance
- Initial stock
- Fit-out of premises
- Specialist computer software; for example architects use 'CAD' (Computer Aided Design) software to help them produce drawings
- Specialist manufacturing equipment, such as a lathe or drill
- Specialist tools; for example woodworking tools if you are operating a furniture-making business

You will also need to consider the cost of having stationery printed for your new business. This might include:

- Business cards
- Paper with your business name and address on it
- Advertising leaflets
- Establishing your own business website

It is important that you also set up some form of record keeping and accounting system, to keep track of cash, receipts, payments, stock levels, profitability and for tax purposes. There are various brands of reasonably priced software to help you do this, such as Sage or Quicken, which are available from office supplies retailers.

If you need to visit your customers from time to time, consider how you will do this. For example, will you need a vehicle? If you don't already have one, or if your family need your existing vehicle to get to work or school, consider purchasing or leasing another vehicle. If you don't want to use up your capital in purchasing a vehicle consider leasing one instead. Leasing means that, in effect, you 'rent' the vehicle by paying a monthly payment to the leasing company; at the end of an agreed term you have the option of purchasing the vehicle for an agreed sum, or simply handing it back to the leasing company. If you are trying to keep your initial costs down (which is always a good idea when first establishing a business) think about ways in which you can manage your business needs without having to obtain another vehicle, either by using public transport to visit your customers, or hiring a vehicle on the occasions when public transport is not a viable option.

If you are going to rent premises you will almost certainly have to provide a cash bond to the owner of the property and perhaps some rent in advance. These amounts also need to be added into the figure for establishment capital. A useful tip here – if you are going to rent or lease premises, do not enter into a long-term agreement with the owner, in case the property turns out to be inappropriate for your business needs; for example, too small, not in the right location, or too big. Remember that once you have entered into a legal contract to rent or lease a property you are bound by that contract and must pay the rent, whether you continue to use the property or not. A short-term contract may not give you certainty of tenancy in the long-term, but it does give you the flexibility to move out should the property prove to be no longer suitable for the needs of your business.

Finally you need to build into your calculation the amount of wages or salary (plus tax) you will require to meet all your personal commitments (such as mortgage payments and living expenses) for the first 12 months of your new business. This figure is included as establishment capital because if the business only generates enough income to cover its trading expenses then it may not be able to afford to pay you the wage you need to meet all your personal commitments. Therefore, it is important that you have sufficient capital to meet these commitments, held in reserve, just in case.

Working Capital

This is the amount of money you will need to keep the business running. Businesses have what is called an Operating Cycle. This means that you start with cash; you then use this cash to purchase (or manufacture) stock; stock is then sold to your customers. When payment is received from your customers you use that cash to purchase or manufacture more stock and the cycle starts over again. The critical point is the time lag between purchasing or manufacturing stock and receiving payment from your customers. Working capital is the cash you will need to cover that gap, allowing you to pay the ongoing expenses of the business until the cash is received from your customers.

It is worth noting at this stage a phrase which should be at the forefront of your mind at all times when you are running a business. It is '**Cash is King**'. The main reason businesses fail is lack of cash, as opposed to lack of profit. Profit is a paper measure of how much you make on a particular transaction. For example, you might sell something for £100 which it has cost you £50 to make so your profit is £50. However, until you have actually been paid by your customer for that transaction the cash you have received is nil, so you have nothing with which to pay your own bills and expenses. This is why it is vital that you ensure your customers pay you promptly because the longer the period between you selling them something and them actually paying you, the greater the amount of working capital you will need to finance the ongoing expenses of your business.

Cashflow Forecast

To work out how much working capital you will need you should prepare a cashflow forecast. An example of such a forecast is included as Appendix 3 to this book. A computer spreadsheet is an ideal vehicle for preparing a forecast because it can be set up so that all the calculations are automatically performed by the computer program. This saves a huge amount of time when you want to run 'What If?' scenarios, changing individual figures in the forecast and seeing what effect it has on the result. Alternatively, if you don't have a computer or don't feel confident using a computer spreadsheet then paper copies of blank cashflow forecasts can usually be obtained from your bank.

Two of the key assumptions to feed into your forecast are, firstly, the time period you will allow your customers before they pay you and, secondly, the time period your suppliers will allow you before you have to pay them. These are called 'credit given days' and 'credit taken days'. For example, you may sell something today on 30-day terms with your customer. Therefore that customer now has 30 days before they have to pay you. Sometimes they may take more than the 30 days; therefore you need to build all of these possibilities into your cashflow forecast, so that you can see how much working capital you will need to see you through that period before you receive payment from your customer.

Often suppliers to new businesses are reluctant to provide long credit terms so try to ensure that you keep the credit terms you offer your customers to a minimum also. Let's look at a couple of examples which will highlight the importance of getting this aspect of your business right:

Example One

A business receives 30-day credit terms from its suppliers and offers 90-day terms to its customers. In this instance the business will have to pay out cash for its initial stock at least 60 days before it is due to receive any cash itself. In addition, if it purchases a second amount of stock from its suppliers, it may also have to pay for this before receiving any payment from its customers. The cashflow of this business, therefore, has to allow for the cost of two purchases of stock in its working capital and this will almost certainly put its cashflow under pressure from the very outset.

Example Two

This business receives 30-day credit terms from its suppliers and offers 15-day terms to its customers. In this instance the business will actually have cash coming in from its customers before it has to pay cash out to its suppliers, and thus will be in a much stronger position cash-wise.

Once you have completed a cashflow forecast this will reveal what your working capital requirements are. The forecast bank balance will be either positive or negative and any negative position has to be covered by either borrowing from a bank or family or by injection of capital by you into the business. It is recommended that you run various 'What If?' scenarios with your cashflow forecast so that you can see what the worst scenario looks like. If you base your cashflow requirements on this worst scenario then you will always have a safety net if your business performs better than this.

4

The Initial Setting-Up of Your Business

Once you have established that your idea is feasible and that you have sufficient finance to set up the business and run it, you can then move forward to actually setting it up. The first thing you will have to decide is what legal form your business will take. The most common forms are a **sole trader**, a **partnership** or a **limited company**. All of these legal forms have advantages and disadvantages and we will now look at each in turn. Some of the advantages and disadvantages relate to taxation and it is important that you seek professional advice on these matters from a qualified accountant.

Sole Trader

This is the simplest form of business legal entity. Essentially it means that you as an individual have decided to run a business for which you are solely responsible. You will be taxed as an individual and you are personally liable for any debts the business incurs.

The advantages of this business form are simplicity, low establishment costs and, depending on the level of profit you expect to make, there may be taxation advantages because of tax allowances which individuals can utilise.

The disadvantages are that taxation may be higher than, for example, a limited company, especially if your profit is large. The main disadvantage however is the fact that you will be personally liable for any debts the business incurs. This means that should the business fail, your creditors can pursue you personally for money owing to them. This could involve the loss of personal assets such as your home or car.

Partnership

This is where two or more persons join together to set up and run a business. Usually they will draw up a Partnership Agreement which will set out, amongst other things, how the business will be run, how profits will be distributed and the circumstances under which the partnership can be dissolved. It is vital that such an agreement is drawn up at the outset, to prevent disputes in the future. All partners are considered by law to be jointly and severally (i.e. individually) liable for the debts of the partnership (see below).

The advantages of this business form are that it is relatively simple compared to a limited company, and the establishment costs are relatively low. Also, any losses from the partnership can be offset against the other taxable income (if any) of the partners.

The disadvantages are that taxation becomes more complex than for a sole trader and that all partners are jointly and severally liable for the debts of the partnership. This means that if the partnership fails, the creditors of the partnership can pursue all or any of the partners for the full amount owing to them. This could involve a partner losing personal assets such as a house or car. For example, if a partnership failed and one partner disappeared, the remaining partner or partners would still be liable for the full debts of the partnership. The main disadvantage of a partnership, however, is that if at some time in the future the partners cannot agree on the way forward for the business this usually means the business will fail, not only because a stalemate situation has been reached but because while the disagreement is going on, the focus on running the business will be lost. This often leads to the business being seriously damaged or failing.

Limited Company

This is where one or more shareholders or owners set up a company to run the business. The company is a separate legal entity from the shareholders or owners. This provides some protection for the individuals in the event of the business failing, unlike a sole trader or partnership.

The advantages of this business form are that it does provide some protection for the individual shareholders or owners in the event of the business failing. (It is to be stressed however that a limited company does not provide full protection to the individuals if, for example, they are proven to be negligent in their running of the business, to the detriment of creditors.) The other advantage is that where the profit of the business is expected to be large, then a limited company can offer some taxation advantages over a sole trader or partnership.

The disadvantages of this business form are that establishment costs are higher than for a sole trader or partnership, because you will need the services of an accountant to help you set up a company. The company also has to be registered with Companies House, for which fees are payable. Ongoing costs are also higher because the company will be required to submit an annual return plus a copy of its annual accounts (or an abbreviated version in the case of a small company) to Companies House and pay the appropriate annual fee for doing this. Details of these fees can be found on the Companies House website, at the address shown in the Useful Addresses section at the end of this book. Companies House also lays down very strict guidelines for directors of companies which must be followed at all times. Failure to do so can lead to heavy fines or imprisonment. Companies House runs seminars around the country for new company directors. If you are planning to set up as a limited company I would recommend that you take advantage of one of these seminars, so that you fully understand your obligations as a director. A further disadvantage of limited companies is that taxation issues can be more complex and the regular services of an accountant will probably be required. This adds to the costs of running the business.

There are other types of business structure, but these are often very complex. For someone establishing a business for the first time it is best to choose from the three main types of structure, as set out above. An accountant can advise you on the best structure for your particular business.

Business Name

If you intend to operate as a sole trader or a partnership you are allowed to do so in your own name. Alternatively you may decide to trade under a business name. If you intend to trade as a limited company you must register the company name at Companies House. Your accountant can help you do this.

When choosing a name for your business, there are certain guidelines which you must bear in mind:

- The business name must not be offensive
- It should not use sensitive words or expressions
- If you are trading as a sole trader or partnership then you cannot have the words 'limited' or 'plc' (or equivalents) in the name because only limited companies can use these words and you might therefore be misleading people into thinking that you are trading as a limited company when in fact you are not

- You should not use a name which is already in use by another business. If you are a sole trader and someone else has the same name and lives at the other end of the country from you, then this should not be a problem. However, if someone living close by is already trading under the same name then you should try to use a different trading name

VAT

If the annual turnover (sales) of your business is £61,000 or more, or if you expect to generate sales of greater than £61,000 over the next 30 days (figures current at time of writing), then you need to register for VAT unless your business is VAT exempt (see below). If your annual turnover is less than £61,000 then you are not required to register for VAT but you may choose to do so voluntarily. The advantages of registering voluntarily are that you can then reclaim some of the VAT you pay on purchases for your business (machinery, stock etc) and also your business will have increased credibility – if your customers see that you are charging VAT they will get the impression that you are a serious business and may feel more comfortable in dealing with you. The main disadvantage of voluntary registration for VAT is that it will involve you in extra paperwork, maintaining records of VAT received and paid, and submitting regular VAT returns to HM Revenue & Customs.

Certain types of goods and services are exempt from VAT, such as insurance and certain types of educational and training services. If your business will only be supplying goods or services which are VAT-exempt then you do not need to register for VAT.

Once you have registered for VAT you must add VAT at the prevailing rate to all your sales invoices. There are currently 3 different rates of VAT: 17.5%, 5% and 0%. Have a look at the HM Revenue & Customs website to find out which will apply to your business (address in the Useful Addresses section at the end of this book).

If you are registered for VAT, you are required to submit a VAT return to HM Revenue & Customs at regular intervals, usually quarterly. This return summarises all the VAT you have received and paid during the quarter. If you have received more VAT than you have paid you must send the excess amount to HM Revenue & Customs. For example, if you have received VAT amounting to £10,000 during the quarter and have paid out VAT amounting to £7,500 then you will need to send the balance of £2,500 to HM Revenue & Customs. Conversely, if you have paid more VAT than you have received then the excess balance is due to you from HM Revenue & Customs.

In my experience over the years as a bank manager, the paying of VAT owing to HM Revenue & Customs is one of the most common causes of businesses experiencing cashflow problems. The reason for this is that businesses receive VAT when they make sales but often the owner then spends that money on purchasing items for their business, for example stock, or spending the money on themselves, for example buying a new car. Consequently, when the time falls due to pay the VAT to HM Revenue & Customs, the business does not have the cash to do so, leaving the business owner open to potential action and fines for non-payment. It is important to remember therefore that VAT received is not all yours to spend – you must account to HM Revenue & Customs for it at the appropriate time. One solution I used to suggest to customers was that they open a separate bank account for VAT and when they receive money from their customers they deposit the VAT element into that separate account. This meant that they didn't spend the money on other things and that they always had the funds available when the VAT payment fell due.

VAT returns can be submitted electronically via the HM Revenue & Customs website and if you owe VAT to HM Revenue &

Customs you must pay it within 1 month of each quarter end. For example, for the quarter ending 31st March any VAT owing must be paid by 30th April. For more details about VAT generally, submitting returns electronically, help for small businesses, and the prevailing rates of VAT, have a look at the HM Revenue & Customs website (address in the Useful Addresses section at the end of this book).

One of the problems small businesses find with VAT is that under the normal method of accounting for VAT, a business must account for all items, whether paid or not. In other words, they may have to remit VAT to HM Revenue & Customs on an invoice which has not yet actually been paid by its customer. For example, you may have sold some goods to a customer for £10,000 which will attract VAT of £1,750 (at the standard rate of 17.5%). If at the end of the quarter your customer has still not actually paid you, you are still required to pay the VAT of £1,750 to HM Revenue & Customs. You will see that this can have a significant impact on your cashflow. However, small businesses obtain help from HM Revenue & Customs with this issue in that if the annual turnover of a business is no more than £660,000 (figure current at time of writing) it can account for VAT on a cash basis. Under the cash accounting scheme you only account for VAT on the basis of cash actually received or paid. For example, if you have issued an invoice to a customer but it has not been paid, then you do not account for this amount until it has been paid.

A further scheme which HM Revenue & Customs offers to businesses to assist in 'smoothing out' VAT obligations is called the Annual Accounting Scheme. Under this scheme you can make monthly or quarterly instalments to HM Revenue & Customs based on an estimate of your total annual VAT liability. Then, at the end of the year, you submit one return and pay or receive any balance due, based on what your actual VAT liability is and what you have already paid in instalments during the year.

This is particularly useful for budgeting purposes because you know in advance what your monthly or quarterly instalment will be. Also, it saves you some time because you only have to submit one return per year instead of the usual four. The main disadvantage with this scheme is that if your business usually receives repayment of VAT from HM Revenue & Customs, you will have to wait a whole year for your money. To qualify for the Annual Accounting Scheme your business must have expected annual turnover (sales) of less than £1,350,000 (figure current at time of writing).

Taxation

All businesses are required to submit an annual tax return, whether they are a company, partnership or a sole trader. The return will detail your taxable income for the year and the amount of tax due on that income. From your second year of trading, HM Revenue & Customs will require you to make payments on account for tax. This will be an estimate of how much tax you will need to pay for the current year, based on your tax return from the previous year. For example, if you had a tax liability of £5000 last year then HM Revenue and Customs will probably require you to make payments on account totalling £5000 in the current year. You will normally be expected to make two payments during the year, on 31st January and 31st July. When you submit your tax return at the end of the year, the payments on account you have made will go towards your tax liability for the year.

Taxation is a complex subject and tax laws change regularly, so it is important to seek the advice and support of a qualified accountant in relation to all your tax matters, even if you are a small business. Ask friends who are already in business to recommend an accountant to you. Alternatively, have a look in Yellow Pages or contact the Institute of Chartered Accountants (website address in the Useful Addresses section at the end of this book).

If you operate your business from home you may be able to claim a proportion of your household expenses as a taxable deduction. This may include a proportion of costs such as electricity, gas, water and telephone. As a general rule, you will be able to claim these in proportion to the space your business occupies at your home. For example, if you use one room solely for business purposes and this room is equivalent to 10% of your total home area then you will be able to claim 10% of your electricity, gas, water etc. For more guidance on this matter, refer to the publications produced by HM Revenue & Customs, or speak to your accountant. Remember that you may be called upon to substantiate your claims, so make sure that you keep appropriate records. By law you are required to keep tax records for a minimum of 5 years from the date of your financial year end.

National Insurance

National Insurance goes towards paying for our state pension, healthcare and other state benefits. Self-employed people generally pay two classes of National Insurance contributions – Class 2 and Class 4. Class 2 contributions are generally paid by all self-employed people, except those on low incomes or of state pension age, while Class 4 contributions are only payable if your profits (not income) reach a certain figure (£5,225 per annum at time of writing).

Class 2 contributions are currently set at a weekly rate of £2.20 and can be paid to HM Revenue & Customs either monthly or quarterly. If your income from self-employment is less than £4,635 per annum (figure correct at time of writing), or you are of state pension age (currently 60 for women and 65 for men), you can apply for a certificate of exception from HM Revenue & Customs.

Class 4 contributions are payable based upon your annual profit. HM Revenue & Customs can tell you how much you need to pay, or you can use the free calculator on the BusinessLink website (address in the Useful Addresses section at the end of this book).

If you are employing people you must deduct National Insurance contributions (Class 1) from their pay and remit it to HM Revenue & Customs. We will look at this requirement later in this chapter under 'Employing staff'.

Pensions

Everyone needs to plan ahead for retirement, even those who are setting up their own business. We are living longer and healthier lives, so it is even more important to think about saving for retirement. Whilst you may be thinking that you will sell your business when you decide to retire and that the money you get from that sale will be your retirement fund, it does not necessarily follow that that will be the way it turns out. What happens, for example, if no one wants to buy your business?

One of the ways in which you can provide for your retirement is through a pension. The basic state pension will give you a start, but to have the lifestyle you want in retirement you need to think about a second pension, and the sooner you start the better.

Unlike employees, while you are self-employed you will not build up an entitlement to the additional state pension (also called the State Second Pension and formerly the State Earnings-Related Pension Scheme, or SERPS). The Class 2 National Insurance contributions you pay when you are self-employed only count towards the basic state pension. Any additional state pension you may have previously built up as an employee is, of course, protected and you will start to receive it when you claim your state pension.

Also, if you are self-employed you cannot join an occupational pension scheme unless you also work for an employer that operates one. But you can join and make payments into what are known as stakeholder and personal pension schemes.

Stakeholder pensions are flexible pension schemes which are offered by a number of providers such as banks, insurance companies and building societies. The key benefit for someone investing in a stakeholder pension scheme is that there is an upper limit on the management charges that can be levied each year by the scheme managers. The stakeholder pension scheme manager or trustees will put your contributions into investments for you, such as stocks and shares. When you retire, you use your fund to buy a pension from a pension scheme provider. By law, stakeholder pensions must meet a number of minimum standards to make sure they offer value for money, flexibility and security. One of the standards is that management charges in each year must not amount to more than the limit set down in law. For people who join a stakeholder pension scheme after 6th April 2005 the limit is a yearly management charge of 1.5% for the first 10 years of membership. If these members stay in the scheme for more than 10 years the annual management charge reduces to 1% from then onwards.

A personal pension is another way of saving for your retirement. You can buy a personal pension plan from financial organisations such as insurance companies, banks and building societies. You usually pay into the personal pension every month and the pension provider invests your money, as with a stakeholder pension. At retirement you can use this money to provide a tax-free lump sum and a secure pension income. The difference between a personal pension and a stakeholder pension is that with a personal pension the annual management charges made by the scheme manager are not subject to regulation by law; therefore they may be higher than those charged under a stakeholder pension scheme.

For more information on pensions, speak to an independent financial advisor (you will find them in Yellow Pages) or have a look at the Government Pension Service website (address in the Useful Addresses section at the end of this book).

Insurance

It is important that you establish adequate insurance cover for all the assets of your business. These assets may include, amongst others, staff, premises, stock, equipment and vehicles.

If you are going to employ people then you are required to take out employer's liability insurance, to provide cover for claims from your employees if they get injured while working for you, or if they contract an illness as a result of working for you.

You should also consider taking out public liability insurance. This covers claims from members of the public – for example visitors to your business – for injury, death or damage to property caused by your business activities.

Many businesses also take out product liability insurance to cover against harm caused by their products or services.

If you are providing professional advice to your customers you should take out professional indemnity insurance. This provides cover in the event of someone making a claim against you for loss suffered as a result of your professional advice, assuming that you are found to be negligent or that you made a mistake in the advice you gave.

If you purchase a business insurance policy from an insurance broker or direct from an insurance company it is likely that it will contain all of the above types of insurance, with the option to leave out those types which do not apply to your particular business.

Last but by no means least, don't forget the most important asset the business has – you. You should consider taking out insurance to protect your income in the event of you not being able to work through ill health or accident. Remember that you no longer work for an employer who may continue to pay you if you have an extended period of sick leave.

If you are running your business from home it is important to remember that your normal home insurance policy will probably not cover you for loss of business equipment or losses caused by business use. Therefore it is important to advise your insurance company of what you intend to do and get them to issue an official notification confirming that they have been advised. In this way there can be no argument at a later date should you need to make a claim.

Licences

Certain types of business require special licences to be able to operate; for example real estate agents and businesses in the building and construction industry. More information on licences can be found on the BusinessLink website (address in the Useful Addresses section at the end of this book). If your business is required to have a licence to operate then you must obtain this before starting to trade.

Planning Permission

You may need planning permission to run a business from a particular location. For example, if you plan to run a restaurant from a property which was previously an estate agent's office, then it is likely that the current planning permission for the property will not cover the retailing of food from the premises. You should check with your local council to see if you need permission to run your business from a particular location. They will also advise you on the process to go through if you do need planning permission.

You may decide to run your business from home. This can have advantages in that costs are minimised when compared to renting premises. However, it is important to check with your local council to see if there are any restrictions on businesses operating from residential premises. It may be that you will require planning permission to operate your business from home and advice should be sought from your local council on this matter.

Bank Account

Your business will need a separate bank account, unless you are operating as a sole trader in which case you can use your private bank account. However, it can get confusing if both private and business transactions are passed through the same account; therefore a separate business account is recommended even if you are a sole trader.

To open a business account the bank will need to positively identify you and also see some evidence of the trading name of the business (if you are using a different trading name to your own name). Examples of the likely documents you will be required to supply are:

- Passport
- Driving licence
- A utility bill, bank or credit card statement, or council tax bill, in order to confirm your address

In addition to the above, if you are using a trading name:

- An example of your business invoice
- A utility bill confirming the trading name and address
- A copy of the business letterhead showing the trading name, registered address and names of the proprietors of the business

Shop around to see what is the best package for your business. Most banks offer special fee arrangements for small businesses, so compare them and decide which will be the best for your business. A bank which provides a lot of support material for small businesses is obviously one which values its small business customers so this may be the one for you. Also consider which is the most convenient bank for you, particularly if you will be receiving cash payments from your customers which need to be paid into the bank. In this case, a bank which has car parking facilities is preferable, so that you do not have to carry the cash too far between your car and the bank.

You will need a cheque book for your business and possibly the facility to receive credit card payments from your customers, if you are going to offer them that payment option. If you do need to have the facility to receive credit card payments, your bank can assist you in setting this up.

Ask your bank for statements of your account to be sent to you at least monthly, so that you can reconcile the account with your business records on a regular basis. A very useful service provided to businesses by banks is online or internet banking. This allows you to view your account 24 hours a day, print statements, transfer money between your accounts and make payments to third parties. You will probably find that once you are running your business you do not have much free time during the day and most of the paperwork side of the business will be done in the evenings. The ability to view your bank account and carry out transactions outside normal office hours is thus extremely useful.

Often people worry about the security of online or internet banking, which the media doesn't help by printing scare-mongering stories each time there is a problem. The fact is that there are millions of electronic banking transactions happening every day and occasionally something goes wrong. However, if you bring it to the attention of your bank straight away they will usually sort it out for you. There are certain precautions you can take though, to ensure that the likelihood of anything happening to you is greatly diminished.

Firstly, never divulge your password to anyone. Owners, partners or directors should all have their own individual passwords for accessing the system and these passwords should not be written down anywhere. Choose something which is easy to remember (a sequence of letters and numbers is best, since words can be guessed by hackers) and commit it to memory.

Secondly, an issue to be aware of is the growing trend today of what is known as 'phishing'. This is where a person receives an email purporting to be from their bank, asking them to confirm their electronic banking details, including their password. **Never respond to these requests.** They are from unscrupulous people who just want to obtain your electronic banking details in order to steal your money. Banks never ask you to divulge your password, so if you receive such a request do not respond.

Thirdly, when you access your bank's online or internet banking system a small padlock symbol will appear in the corner of your web-browser window. This indicates that you are on what is known as a secure site, which is protected from prying eyes by sophisticated security systems. Therefore, you are safe to use this site knowing that your details are secure and that no one else can intercept the data passing between your computer and the bank.

Finally, always ensure that you have anti-virus, spyware detection and personal firewall software loaded onto your computer. This will minimise the risk of someone finding out your electronic banking details and using them to steal money from your account. The software can be purchased from all good computer shops and major office supplies retailers.

Employing Staff

Employing staff is a serious investment. It says that the business is growing and that it wants to continue to grow, as more staff enable more sales to be achieved. However, employing staff is not a matter to be taken lightly and involves serious consideration of a number of issues, such as:

- Can the business afford to pay extra staff?
- Will the business need full-time staff, or would part-time and temporary staff be better options?
- Do the staff need to have certain skills or qualifications?
- What are the legal responsibilities of an employer towards employees?
- What arrangements need to be put in place to pay Tax and National Insurance for employees? How much must be deducted from the wages of employees in Tax and National Insurance?

A good starting point when considering employing staff is to write down a job description for the role to be filled, including any particular skills which will be required. This will help you formulate a job advertisement and provide a basis for the questions you will ask potential candidates at an interview.

Before deciding to make a job offer to a potential employee, consider taking up references for them by contacting their previous employment referees and finding out if they were a good worker, what their role was with that employer, what their attendance record was like etc. Also, if the person you are considering employing has a particular qualification which is essential to the role, then check out that qualification by requesting sight of an original certificate and making further enquiries as appropriate. Finally, if the person will be working with children or vulnerable adults then you should carry out a criminal records check by contacting the Criminal Records Bureau (website address in the Useful Addresses section at the end of this book). It is important to let the potential candidate know that you will be carrying out any checks, in order to comply with the provisions of the Data Protection Act.

If you do decide to employ someone, remember that employees are entitled to receive a written statement of employment within 2 months of their start date. This document sets out the terms and conditions of the employment. Your solicitor can help you draw one of these up or alternatively there is a free version available from the website of BusinessLink (address in the Useful Addresses section at the end of this book).

Once you employ someone, you need to inform HM Revenue & Customs that you are now an employer, and also that you have taken on a new employee. You need to obtain the employee's P45 and National Insurance number so that you can set up the appropriate payroll process and ensure that tax and National Insurance are deducted at the correct rates. HM Revenue & Customs will help you by providing appropriate tables setting out the current rates. They also have a number of Help Lines to assist employers with payroll queries. It is important to remember that if you have employees you need to remit PAYE (tax) deductions and National Insurance contributions to HM Revenue & Customs on the 19th of each month, so you need to set up a payroll system to ensure that all your obligations are fulfilled correctly.

Health and Safety

As a business owner, you have a legal responsibility for the health and safety of your employees (if you have any) and anyone else impacted by the operations of your business, such as customers or people living near to your business premises.

Health and safety is about creating and maintaining a healthy working environment and taking appropriate precautions to prevent people being hurt or becoming ill. Your legal responsibility also extends to protection of the environment, for example ensuring that any waste products from your business do not enter waterways or contaminate the ground.

If you have employees, or if customers and the general public have access to your business premises, you may have to register your business with the appropriate authority. For example, if you operate a car repair business then you have to register with the

Health and Safety Executive. Similarly, if you operate a restaurant or catering business then you must register with your local authority's environmental health and safety department. To check if you need to register your business for health and safety purposes, have a look at the website of the Health and Safety Executive (address in the Useful Addresses section at the end of this book) or talk to your local authority environmental health and safety department.

It is vital that you have a health and safety policy for your business, and if you employ 5 or more people this policy must be in writing. If you are visited by the Health and Safety Executive or your local authority environmental health and safety department you will be required to produce this written policy. Failure to do so can lead to further action for non-compliance with health and safety legislation.

It is also important to keep an accident book, where you record details of all accidents which happen at your business premises, whether it be something as simple as a cut finger or something more serious such as someone falling over.

As a business owner you must carry out regular risk assessments to ensure that your business complies with health and safety regulations. A good starting point is to walk around your business with a notebook, noting down anything which might pose a hazard or risk to yourself, your employees, your customers, or anyone else visiting your business premises. Obvious things which I have noticed when visiting business premises over the years are hazards such as:

- Computer cabling trailing across the floor
- Worn carpet which can trip people up
- Desk drawers left open for people to fall over or bang their legs against
- Employees not wearing protective glasses when working with machinery

- Steps up to or down from a room which are not clearly identified and which might cause someone to fall
- Filing cabinets being filled too full, or not securely fastened to a wall, so that there is a risk of them toppling over when one of the drawers is opened
- People flinging doors open without considering if there might be someone else on the other side

You can see that these examples are really all just common sense, but sometimes people forget and just don't think about the hazards. Being aware yourself, and making your employees aware of the potential dangers is all part of having robust health and safety policies within your business.

It is tempting for a business owner to think that health and safety is a low priority and that their time is better spent getting more sales, or getting work for a customer completed on time. However, you must bear in mind that as a business owner you have a legal responsibility for health and safety within your business, and failure to comply with this legislation can be very expensive, both in terms of fines for non-compliance and also in terms of potential damages awarded against your business if someone is hurt or killed as a result of your failure to apply robust health and safety policies. Businesses do go broke as a result of the financial consequences of poor health and safety standards, but apart from the financial implications it is simply the right thing to do – ensuring that you, your employees, your customers and the environment are kept healthy and safe.

For more information about your health and safety responsibilities have a look at the Health and Safety Executive or BusinessLink websites (addresses in the Useful Addresses section at the end of this book), both of which have helpful checklists to ensure that you cover all of your health and safety responsibilities.

5

Essential Bookkeeping Records

To enable you to gather all the information required to produce annual accounts for your business, and to comply with tax legislation, you will need to keep certain essential bookkeeping records. These will also show you how your business is performing. A lot of people see the word 'bookkeeping' shudder with horror and call in their accountant! But it does not need to be that way, and if you can complete a few basic bookkeeping records yourself you will not only gain a greater understanding of your business, but also save yourself some accountant's fees.

There are four main 'books' or records which a business needs to keep, to maintain financial control of that business. They can all be purchased from any good office stationery suppliers and are relatively inexpensive. Alternatively there are various brands of reasonably priced accounting software such as Sage or Quicken, which are available from office supplies retailers. We will discuss the advantages and disadvantages of using bookkeeping software later in this chapter.

The four main books or records which you should keep are:

- The Sales Ledger
- The Purchases Ledger
- The Cash Book
- The Fixed Asset Register

1. The Sales Ledger

The sales ledger is sometimes also called the debtors ledger, and is a record of all the sales you have made. Details which you should record in the sales ledger typically include the date of the invoice which is created when you make a sale, the amount of the invoice, the customer's name, the amount of VAT, and the date the invoice was paid.

This last point, the date the invoice was paid, is very important because it will enable you at any point in time to see quickly which of your customers has not yet paid you. This will help you to chase those customers for payment.

2. The Purchases Ledger

The purchases ledger is sometimes also called the creditors ledger, and is a record of all the goods and services you have purchased for your business. These can include such items as stock purchases, telephone expenses and stationery purchases. Details which you should record in the purchases ledger typically include the date of the invoice from the supplier, the amount of the invoice, the supplier's name, the amount of VAT, and the date on which the invoice was paid.

This last point, the date the invoice was paid, is important because it will enable you at any point in time to see quickly how much you owe to your suppliers (or creditors) and thus to relate this figure to the amount of cash you have available to pay those invoices. If you don't have sufficient cash to pay all of the invoices, you need to chase up some of your debtors (people who owe you money) and get some cash coming in to your business, to enable you to pay your creditors.

3. The Cash Book

The cash book is used to record the payments and receipts for your business, that is, all the money going in and out. Typically the cash book is divided into receipts on the left-hand side of the page and payments on the right-hand side. Each page has columns to record money passing in and out of your business, and the headings of these columns will be similar to the categories shown in the sample cashflow forecast (see Appendix 3 at the end of this book).

The receipts and payments should be added up each month. The total for the 'Bank' columns should equal the sum of the receipts and payments columns, as appropriate.

Deducting the total of the payments from the total of the receipts will give you the net cash movement for your business in that month. By adding this net cash movement figure to your cash balance carried forward from the **previous** month, you will arrive at the new cash balance at the end of the **current** month. This figure should then be compared to your bank statement to ensure that it matches, after allowing for any outstanding cheques. This process is called reconciliation and is a vital element in monitoring the performance of your business. For more information on this important process, see later in this chapter under 'Bank Reconciliation'.

4. The Fixed Asset Register

Fixed assets are defined as those assets that are owned by your business for long-term use in the business, and not intended for resale. They will include items such as buildings, machinery, motor vehicles and office equipment.

Assets which are not fixed assets include items such as stock. For example a corner shop will hold a stock of goods for resale (tinned food, jars of coffee etc). Because these are intended for resale they are called stock and are not included as fixed assets.

The Fixed Asset Register is where you record details of the fixed assets of your business. You should record the following as a minimum:

- Date of Purchase
- Cost at Purchase Date
- Description (preferably including serial number, make and model number)
- Depreciation attributed in the year (see below)
- Closing Value at the end of each financial year (cost less accumulated depreciation)
- Disposal Date (when appropriate)
- Profit or Loss on the Disposal (generally the amount of money received upon disposal, less the current value of the asset as shown in the fixed asset register). For example, if you sell an asset for £5,000 and the value of that asset in your books is only £4,000 then you will have made a profit of £1,000 on the sale and this figure needs to be recorded in the fixed asset register.

Depreciation is the amount by which an asset of your business is reduced in value each year over the useful life of that asset. For example, a machine might cost you £10,000 and have a useful life of 5 years before you need to replace it. Therefore it would be reasonable to depreciate the machine in your records by £2,000 per year so that at the end of 5 years the machine has a closing value of nil in your records.

Fixed Assets form part of the Balance Sheet of your business, so it is important to have a list of those assets ready for insertion into the Balance Sheet, hence the recording of them in the Fixed Asset Register. We will look at the Balance Sheet in more detail in Chapter 8.

How Often Should These Records Be Completed?

This will vary from business to business but as a general rule the cash book should be completed daily and the sales and purchase ledgers at least weekly. The Fixed Asset Register should be completed as fixed assets are acquired or disposed of, and then at the end of each financial year when you will work out the Closing Value (see above). If the tasks are left any longer than this they will take a long time to complete and become a real chore, whereas by taking just a few minutes each day or week to complete them they will seem much smaller tasks and completion will be easier. Get into the habit of completing these records regularly, so that you don't get behind in your paperwork.

I know that it can be difficult to find the time to keep these records up to date, given the day to day time pressures of running your business. However, they are an essential part of the survival of your business and thus it is time well spent. This is because it cannot be stressed enough that cashflow is probably the major issue which all businesses face, especially new businesses, and it is essential that you know exactly what your business's cash position is at all times. This will help ensure that your business does not run out of cash. If it does, then the business is at severe risk of failure. By regularly completing and maintaining your business's cash and the relative positions of debtors and creditors, you will stand a far greater chance of making your business successful.

Also, having up-to-date, accurate records will save time and money when it comes to your financial year end, when you want to prepare the year end accounts for your tax return. They will also be invaluable if you ever have a visit from the tax authorities. A set of up-to-date, accurate records will go a long way towards impressing them and showing them that you are a serious business person.

Bank Reconciliation

At the end of each month a reconciliation should be carried out (see above under 'The Cash Book') to ensure that your records are accurate. This is sometimes called 'balancing the books' and helps ensure that the cash position of your business is known on a regular basis.

The bank reconciliation involves adding up all the payments into and out of your business and then comparing this to your business bank account to ensure that the net total of cash in or out is the same as the movement in your bank account from one period to the next, ideally on a monthly basis as a minimum. Let's look at a simple example to illustrate the reconciliation process:

Opening cash balance at the beginning of the month (from Cash Book)	£5,500
Plus total receipts for the month (from Cash Book)	£10,000
Minus total payments for the month (from Cash Book)	£7,000
Equals closing cash balance at the end of the month	**£8,500**
Bank balance at the end of the month (from Bank Statement)	£9,200
Less cheques issued but not yet presented (included in Payments above)	£700
Reconciled bank balance at the end of the month	**£8,500**

You can see from the above example that the bank account is now 'reconciled'. That is, the closing cash balance is the same as the reconciled bank balance. If for some reason the two figures are different then you need to check back and find where the error is, otherwise you will be starting next month with an incorrect figure. This will continue as long as you fail to find the error and correctly reconcile the bank account, so it is important that you spend time finding any errors and correcting them.

Bookkeeping Software – Advantages and Disadvantages

There are numerous bookkeeping software programs available from office supplies retailers. They can be a great help in managing the financial records of your business. Let's now have

a look at the advantages and disadvantages of using bookkeeping software.
The main advantages are:

- Bookkeeping can be a complex matter, and a manually created ledger system can be hard to understand for someone who has not had any accountancy training. Computers and bookkeeping software have changed all that and now you don't have to be an accountancy expert to be able to manage the bookkeeping of your business.
- A huge benefit of a computerised bookkeeping system is the ability to compile and see records instantly for whatever period of time you chose. Examples of records you may want to review from time to time are profit and loss accounts (so that you can see how much profit you are making), or balance sheets (so that you can see the value, or net worth, of your business at any point in time). Bookkeeping software will produce these in a format which is easy to understand, not only for you as the business owner but also for your accountant or bank manager, who may want to see how your business is performing if you are approaching him or her for a bank overdraft or loan.
- Proper forward planning is essential to the success of any business, and bookkeeping software can help you prepare budgets and forecasts. Again, if you are approaching your bank manager for an overdraft or loan, he or she will probably want to see a forecast or budget for your business and bookkeeping software can help you to prepare these.
- It is essential to the success of your business to properly monitor who owes you money and amounts you owe to your suppliers. Bookkeeping

software can help you by instantly producing reports of who owes you money and people you owe money to, so that you can see at a glance if there are people you need to chase up for payment or people you are due to pay. This will help you to manage the cashflow of your business.

- Bookkeeping software usually includes a cashflow forecast program, which can help you put together a cash forecast for your business. This will enable you to ensure that you have sufficient cash in your bank account to meet all of your expenses. Alternatively it may give you early warning that you need to approach your bank manager for an overdraft, if your forecast indicates you will need the support of the bank through a lean time. Remember that if it looks like you will need an overdraft, approach them in plenty of time because it can take up to 4-6 weeks to arrange an overdraft facility, so you need to get your request in early.
- The use of bookkeeping software can help ensure you meet your legal obligations to HM Revenue & Customs for items such as VAT. The software can help you to work out quickly how much VAT needs to be paid or refunded, and the forecasting programs can help ensure that you have budgeted for these and therefore have the cash to pay the VAT (if you are a net payer of VAT) to HM Revenue & Customs when the payment falls due. In this way you will avoid any fines which may apply to late payment, or legal action for non-payment.
- Stock control is made easier by the use of bookkeeping software. Many businesses waste money buying surplus amounts of stock simply because they are not aware of how much stock they have, how much they need, and what their minimum

required stock levels are. Bookkeeping software can help you monitor and budget for stock so that your stock levels are always kept at the optimum for your business. Remember that to acquire stock you need to pay money for it. Therefore it can sometimes be helpful to view stock sitting on your shelves as piles of cash. This often concentrates the mind on keeping stock levels to a minimum!

- Computerised bookkeeping systems allow you to data-mine the information in the system, to inform you which products and customers make you the most profit. Conversely, they can also highlight any unprofitable products which you may want to cease producing.
- Most bookkeeping software enables you to reconcile your bank account with your accounting records automatically, thus reducing the amount of time spent carrying out a bank reconciliation.

The main disadvantages of using bookkeeping software are:

- As with any computer program, it relies on the user entering accurate information. If you input inaccurate information, or if you don't keep the data up to date, the software will not produce useful information for you.
- You need to remember to keep a backup copy of your information, in case your computer fails or is stolen – you don't want to have to go back and recreate months and months of records if something happens to your main files!

VAT Records

We cannot leave this chapter on essential bookkeeping records without mentioning VAT records. Whilst not fundamentally linked to the profit and loss account or balance sheet of your business, it is essential that you maintain VAT records and account to HM Revenue & Customs for VAT accordingly.

The only way in which VAT might form part of the balance sheet of your business is to record any amounts outstanding to or from HM Revenue & Customs at your financial year end. Amounts owing to HM Revenue & Customs will be shown under Creditors and amounts owing to you by HM Revenue & Customs under Debtors.

We looked at VAT in more detail in Chapter 4, so go back now and refresh your memory if you are unsure about your VAT obligations.

Summary

At this stage you may be asking yourself, 'Why do I have to keep and complete all of these records?' Well, apart from the legal requirement to do so for taxation purposes, all of the records we have talked about in this chapter are used as the basis, or building blocks, for creating the accounting records for your business, such as the profit and loss account and the balance sheet. We will now look at these accounting records in more detail, together with some basics of accounting.

6

Some Accounting Basics

Accounting is a system for measuring business activity and converting that information into reports of various kinds, such as the Profit and Loss Account and the Balance Sheet.

These reports are known as Financial Statements or Financial Accounts (or sometimes just 'Accounts') and are used to record how a business is performing. In turn these Financial Accounts are used by the owner(s) of a business to understand how their business is performing and also for showing to third parties who may want that information, such as bank managers when they are approached for an overdraft or loan. The Financial Accounts are also used to help prepare your annual tax return.

Bookkeeping is a fundamental part of the accounting process and while there are numerous accounting software packages available which can do a lot of the hard work for you (see Chapter 5), it is important that you have at least a basic knowledge of how accounting works. Armed with this knowledge you will be in a better position to manage the financial aspects of your business and also to make informed decisions about financial questions: for example whether you should take on extra staff, open a new outlet or move to bigger premises.

The fundamental theory behind accounting is that every transaction has a dual impact in the financial records of a business. This is called **double-entry bookkeeping**.

Double-Entry Bookkeeping

The origins of a primitive double-entry system have been traced as far back as the 12th Century, and by the end of the 15th Century the merchants in Venice used the system widely. Luca Pacioli, a monk and collaborator of Leonardo da Vinci, first codified the system in a mathematics textbook in 1494. Pacioli is often called the 'father of accounting' because he was the first to publish a detailed description of the double-entry system, which enabled others to study and use it. The system has changed remarkably little since then.

Double-entry bookkeeping is a system which accounts for every aspect of a transaction – where it came from and where it went to. In other words, each transaction has a dual impact in the financial records (or accounts) of a business. This 'from' and 'to' aspect of a transaction is referred to by the term 'double-entry'. Let's look at a couple of examples to illustrate this:

Example 1

You are running your business and you decide to take £10,000 out of your bank account to purchase some stock. The two entries in your accounts would be:

- Cash at bank reduces by £10,000
- Stock held increases by £10,000

It is said that the transaction now 'balances' because two entries have been made, one showing where the transaction came from and one showing where it has gone to.

Example 2

You carry out the same transaction as in Example 1, except that this time your supplier gives you 30 days credit on your purchase of stock. In other words, you don't have to pay your supplier now; instead you will pay them in 30 days' time. The two initial entries in your accounts would be:

- Stock held increases by £10,000 (as in Example 1)
- Creditors increases by £10,000 (Creditors are amounts your business owes to other parties, such as suppliers)

In due course, when your 30 days' credit expires and you actually pay your supplier, the two entries would be:

- Cash at Bank decreases by £10,000
- Creditors decreases by £10,000

This then is the fundamental theory behind double-entry bookkeeping – each transaction having a dual impact on the accounts of a business, showing where it came from and where it went to.

The Profit and Loss Account

The profit and loss account is sometimes referred to as an income and expenditure statement. Some people find it helpful to think in terms of income and expenditure instead of profit and loss, although strictly speaking they are not entirely the same thing. For the purposes of this book I will use the term profit andloss account.

The profit and loss account documents sales revenue (sometimes called turnover) and all expenditure associated with earning that revenue for the period specified, usually annually although you can also produce weekly, monthly, quarterly and half-yearly profit and loss accounts. Ultimately, the profit and loss account shows how profitable your business is. We will look at the profit and loss account in more detail in Chapter 7.

The Balance Sheet

The balance sheet is a snapshot of the assets and liabilities of your business at a given point in time. For example, if the annual accounts of your business are completed as at 31st March each year then the balance sheet will reflect the assets and liabilities of your business as at that date.

The balance sheet shows the financial strength of the business; the extent to which it is solvent (in other words, by how much the assets exceed the liabilities); how the business is financed; and how quickly its assets can be turned into cash. The general rule is that if an asset can be turned into cash within a period of 12 months it is called a current asset. Generally these will be items such as debtors or stock. If an asset is more long-term in nature, that is more than 12 months, it is called a non-current asset, for example motor vehicles, plant and machinery, or office equipment.

Assets are items which are owned by your business (such as motor vehicles) or are owing to your business (such as money owed to you by your customers – sometimes called debtors or receivables).

Liabilities are items which your business owes to others. These may include monies owing to your suppliers (called creditors) or loans owing to other parties (such as bank loans and hire purchase loans) or monies owing to you (the owner), either by way of loans, or funds you have invested in the business.

The key thing to remember is that a balance sheet must always balance – that is why it is called a balance sheet. When we use the term 'balance' we mean that the total of the assets of the business must always equal the total of the liabilities (including the amount you have invested in the business). Let's have a look at a simple balance sheet to illustrate this fact:

Balance Sheet of XYZ Business as at 31 March XXXX

Current Assets (A)	
Cash	£ 5,000
Debtors	£ 15,000
Stock	£ 10,000
	£ 30,000
Non Current Assets (B)	
Plant & Machinery	£ 10,000
Motor Vehicles	£ 5,000
Office Equipment	£ 1,000
	£ 16,000
Total Assets (A + B = C)	**£ 46,000**
Current Liabilities (D)	
Creditors	£ 5,000
Non Current Liabilities (E)	
Long-Term Loans	£ 25,000
Total Liabilities (D + E = F)	**£ 30,000**
Net Assets (C - F)	**£ 16,000**
Owner's Equity (G)	**£ 16,000**

You can see from the example that the total of the assets is £46,000 (total 'C'). Similarly, the total of the liabilities (including owner's equity which is also a liability of the business because it is funds owing to the owner) is also £46,000 (total of 'F' and 'G'). Therefore the balance sheet is said to 'balance'. We will look at the balance sheet in more detail in Chapter 8.

The Statement of Cashflow and the Cashflow Forecast

Larger businesses often prepare a statement of cashflow which they then include in their annual accounts. This shows the movements of cash into and out of the business during the last year.

Smaller businesses often do not prepare a statement of cashflow. However, what is important is that they prepare a cashflow **forecast**, which is a forecast of cash in and out of the business looking forward. This is a vital management tool because it will show you if you expect to have enough cash coming into your business to meet all of the expected, or forecast, cash payments out of your business. Whilst it is only a forecast of what you expect to happen, given certain assumptions as to the level of sales you hope to make and the expenditure you expect to incur in making those sales, it does at least provide you with a vital forward-looking plan of how much cash your business may need during the year. This will give you early warning of any potential cashflow shortages, thus giving you the opportunity to take action to prevent this or to approach a bank for an overdraft facility to cover the position. We will look at the cashflow forecast in more detail in Chapter 10 – Forecasting the Financial Performance of Your Business.

Summary

This chapter has concentrated on giving you a brief overview of the basics of accounting and some of the reports that are produced. In the next two chapters we will look at the Profit and Loss Account and the Balance Sheet in more detail, as these two reports are arguably the most important ones you will use to demonstrate how your business is performing.

7

The Profit & Loss Account

As we have already seen in Chapter 6, the profit and loss account is sometimes referred to as an income and expenditure statement, but for the purposes of this book I will use the term profit and loss account. Let's now have a look at the profit and loss account in detail, seeing what is included in it, what is not included in it and what it looks like.

What Is Included in the Profit and Loss Account

You will remember from Chapter 6 that the profit and loss account documents sales revenue (sometimes called turnover) and all expenditure associated with earning that revenue for the period specified, usually annually (although you can also produce weekly, monthly, quarterly and half-yearly profit and loss accounts). Ultimately, the profit and loss account shows how profitable your business is.

The expenditure items will include such things as wages, salaries, depreciation, heating and lighting costs, telephone costs etc. Have a look at the example profit and loss account in Appendix 4 now, to get a better understanding of what sort of items it includes.

What Is Not Included in the Profit and Loss Account

Items which are not included in the profit and loss account are those items which belong in the balance sheet of your business (see Chapter 8 – The Balance Sheet). It is sometimes helpful to think of the balance sheet as the register of the assets and liabilities of your business, as distinct from income and expenditure, which is shown in the profit and loss account. The balance sheet will include such items as Debtors (amounts owing to your business by your customers), Creditors (amounts your business owes to other people, for example suppliers), Fixed Assets of your business (for example Property, Plant and Equipment, and Motor Vehicles) and Other Liabilities of your business (for example Bank Loans and Overdrafts). More on these and other balance sheet items later, in Chapter 8.

What does a Profit and Loss Account look like?

Appendix 4 shows what a typical profit and loss account looks like and the items it records. You can see that it details the sales revenue of your business and the expenditure associated with the running of the business. Once all the expenditure is deducted from the sales revenue figure (or gross profit figure if you have 'cost of goods sold' in your business – see below under 'How to Get Started') you are left with what is called the 'Net Profit' of your business. If the net profit figure is a negative number then your business has made a net loss – something to be avoided if at all possible!

How to Get Started

It might be helpful to keep Appendix 4 open in front of you as we go through this next section.

The starting point in compiling a profit and loss account is the sales revenue for the period you are looking at. The next item to consider is 'cost of goods sold'. This item usually only applies if you are carrying stock as part of your business. For example, if your business is selling tyres you would carry stocks of tyres. If you simply supply services, for example secretarial services, you are unlikely to carry stock for resale and therefore cost of goods sold will not really apply. The formula for working out cost of goods sold is:

Opening Stock + Purchases of Stock - Closing Stock = Cost of Goods Sold

If your business is manufacturing something and you employ labour which is directly involved in the manufacturing process, then you may also include that labour cost in cost of goods sold. The reason for this is that the labour is **directly related** to the manufacturing process. This is sometimes also referred to as 'Direct Labour Costs'. Generally, you will only include labour in cost of goods sold if you are manufacturing something. Otherwise labour costs are included in the general expenditure section of the profit and loss account (usually under 'wages' or 'salaries'). Direct labour costs are also known as a variable cost; that is, a cost which varies directly depending on the level of sales. More on variable costs later.

Once you have your cost of goods sold figure, you deduct this from your sales revenue to arrive at what is known as your gross profit. This is an important figure for your business and we will discuss it further under 'Useful Ratios' later in this chapter.

The next step is to list all of the expenditure you incur in running your business. Often there are so many individual expenditure items that it would be impractical to list every one individually. Therefore it is acceptable to group these together under categories, for example 'Light, Heat and Power' might include payments for electricity and gas, rather than showing electricity and gas separately. Remember though that you must keep accurate records of all payments and these must add up to the total shown in your profit and loss account.

Most of the items shown in the example profit and loss account are self explanatory, but it is worth mentioning just a few which require a bit of explanation:

Depreciation

The value of a business asset which provides a benefit to your business over a number of years (for example plant and machinery) declines over the asset's effective life. Using the plant and machinery example, the plant or machinery might give you a number of years of service then be obsolete or worn out. Therefore you are allowed to show a depreciation allowance in your profit and loss account for the decline in value of that asset.

For example, if you purchased a machine costing £100,000 and expected it to have a useful life of 10 years, then it would be reasonable to depreciate the asset at the rate of £10,000 per annum, so that at the end of 10 years the asset would have a nil value in the books of your business. This is a simple example and your accountant will give you more guidance on the exact amount of depreciation you can show in your profit and loss account.

However, you need to remember that depreciation is not allowable for tax purposes, where a capital allowance may be claimed instead. Again, your accountant will advise you how much you can claim.

Interest Paid

This refers to the interest you pay to a bank or finance company on an overdraft, loan or hire purchase agreement. It is only the interest payment you show here, not the principal element of any repayment you make. For example, if you have a bank loan and this is repayable over 5 years in regular monthly instalments, your monthly repayment will include an element to cover interest and an element to cover principal, so that the one monthly repayment will completely repay the loan over the 5 year period.

It is only the interest element which you show in your profit and loss account.

Motor Vehicle Expenses

Remember that you can only claim expenses which relate to the running of your business. Any private element of motor vehicle expenses cannot be claimed.

Useful Ratios

There are some very useful ratios which come out of the profit and loss account. These can help you to manage your business better and help improve its profitability. Let's now have a look at some of the more useful ones:

Gross Profit Percentage

We mentioned earlier that gross profit is calculated as:

Sales - Cost of Goods Sold = Gross Profit

If you then calculate the gross profit figure as a percentage of sales (Gross Profit divided by Sales, multiplied by 100) you obtain the gross profit percentage. This figure can help you in a number of ways:

1. As you monitor the performance of your business, one of the key ratios to concentrate on is the gross profit percentage. The reason for this is that if this percentage is falling it means you are making less profit on your sales and ultimately if this trend continues you may not make enough profit to cover all your expenditure, resulting in the business making a loss.

2. Conversely, if you can increase your gross profit percentage either by increasing your sales price or reducing your cost of goods sold (or both), then you will increase the profit your business makes (assuming that your other expenditure stays the same).

3. The Gross Profit percentage can also help when you are preparing business forecasts. When preparing a forecast you will estimate the value of sales you are expecting to make. By then applying the gross profit percentage your business is achieving, you will immediately know the amount of gross profit you are forecasting. This can save time trying to work out in detail your forecast cost of goods sold. More on forecasting later, in Chapter 10.
4. The other area in which the gross profit percentage is useful is when working out what is known as 'Breakeven'.

Breakeven

This is defined as the minimum level of sales needed to cover all your expenditure. It is an extremely useful tool for managing a business because it allows you to understand the minimum level of sales you need to generate in order to cover a given expenditure total.

The formula for breakeven is:

Total expenditure divided by gross profit % = breakeven sales level

You can also use this formula to carry out 'What If?' analyses – changing the total expenditure figure and recalculating the minimum level of sales you will need to achieve to cover that new level of expenditure. For example, you may decide to move to new premises where the rent for those premises is greater than you are currently paying. You can add the additional rent onto the existing total expenditure for your business, which will give you a new total expenditure figure. Divide this total by the gross profit percentage and you now know what level of sales you need to generate to meet all your planned expenditure. Let's look at an example in detail, using the increased rent scenario:

Current Situation

Sales	£ 500,000
Cost of Goods Sold	£ 250,000
Gross Profit	£ 250,000
Gross Profit %	50%
Total Expenditure	£ 250,000
Net Profit (in this case breakeven)	£0

Proposed Situation, with increased rent of £50,000

Total Expenditure now	£ 300,000
Divided by Gross Profit %	50%
Minimum required sales now	£ 600,000

You can see from the above example that to cover your new increased expenditure total of £300,000 your business will need to generate an additional £100,000 of sales, based on your gross profit percentage of 50%. You would therefore need to decide if you think your business can achieve this increased sales level before deciding whether to move to the new premises.

8

The Balance Sheet

As we have already seen in Chapter 6, the balance sheet is a snapshot of your business at a given point in time. For example, if your annual accounts are completed as at 31st March each year then the balance sheet will reflect the assets and liabilities of your business as at that date.

Assets are items which are owned by your business (such as motor vehicles) or are owing to your business (such as money owed to you by your customers – sometimes called debtors or receivables).

Liabilities are items which your business owes to others. These may include monies owing to your suppliers (called creditors) or loans owing to other parties (such as bank loans and hire purchase loans).

Let's now have a look at the balance sheet in detail, seeing what is included, what is not included and what a balance sheet looks like.

What Is Included in the Balance Sheet

Items which are included in the balance sheet of your business will be those such as Debtors (amounts owing to your business by your customers); Creditors (amounts your business owes to other people, for example suppliers); Fixed Assets of your business (for example Property, Plant and Equipment, and Motor

Vehicles); and Other Liabilities of your business (for example Bank Overdrafts and Loans and Hire Purchase Loans). Have a look at the example Balance Sheet in Appendix 5 now, to get a better understanding of what a balance sheet looks like and what sort of items it includes. The items shown in the example are not exhaustive, but if you apply the rule that any assets and liabilities need to be shown here then you won't go far wrong. We will have a look at the structure of a balance sheet later in this chapter.

What Is Not Included in the Balance Sheet

Items which are not included in the balance sheet are those items which belong in the profit and loss account. As seen in Chapter 7, the profit and loss account documents sales revenue (sometimes called turnover) and all expenditure associated with earning that revenue, such as wages, salaries, depreciation, heating and lighting costs, telephone costs etc. All of these items are included in the profit and loss account, not the balance sheet.

What Does a Balance Sheet Look Like?

You can see from the example balance sheet in Appendix 5 that the assets and liabilities of a business are listed separately, with total liabilities being deducted from total assets to arrive at the net assets of your business. The net assets are also sometimes called the Owner's Equity and show the net position of your business once all the liabilities have been taken away from all the assets. If your business has a negative owner's equity – that is, the total liabilities are greater than the total assets – then this is not a good thing because it is saying that your business does not have sufficient assets to meet all its liabilities. If this is the case, you should seek professional advice immediately from a suitably qualified person (such as an accountant) because there can be serious legal ramifications for you personally if you continue to trade knowing that your business does not have sufficient assets to meet all its liabilities.

You will also see from the example balance sheet that assets and liabilities are sub-divided into 'Current' and 'Non-Current'. The general rule of thumb which applies is that anything which is receivable or realisable (in the case of assets) or payable (in the case of liabilities) within the next 12 months is classed as 'current'. Everything else is classed as 'non-current'. For example, if you have business premises such as a factory in your balance sheet, this is something you intend to keep for a long time so it is classed as a non-current asset. Conversely, stock which you expect to sell in the near future is classed as a current asset.

Useful Ratios

There are some very useful ratios which come out of the balance sheet, such as gearing and liquidity. These can help you manage your business better and assist in improving its financial strength. We will look at these and other key ratios in more detail in Chapter 11.

9

Understanding the Difference Between Cashflow and Profit

Many people who start up their own business do not understand the difference between cashflow and profit. They mistakenly believe that they are one and the same thing. This is a big mistake. It is vital for the well-being of your business that you understand the difference. Let's have a look at what each one means and then explore why they are different and why it is important to understand the difference between the two.

Cashflow

Cashflow is the amount of cash actually received into and paid out of your business. For example, you sell something to a customer and give them an invoice. It is only when they actually pay you that this becomes cashflow into your business. Similarly, you purchase something from a supplier and they will give you an invoice. It is only when you actually pay that invoice that this becomes cashflow out of your business.

Cashflow is arguably the most important issue to be addressed when running a business, not only in the early days but throughout its entire lifetime.

You should be always managing your cashflow. As you get into the day-to-day running of your business it is very easy to forget the importance of cashflow because you will be preoccupied with sales, production, stock purchasing, employee considerations and so on. However, business people ignore cashflow issues at their peril. If not managed appropriately, it will be the undoing of your business.

You should consider the terms of payment you will offer to your customers, being mindful of the terms you are receiving from your suppliers and the amount of cash needed to keep the business running; for example wages, rent, heat, light and power, and telephone costs. It is not good business practice to offer extended payment terms to a customer just to get their business – it is no use 'buying' sales if you end up not getting paid by your customer, because no amount of sales invoiced can replace actual cash received, in terms of helping to pay your business expenses. It is also important that for large amounts of money you don't provide credit to your customers without first checking them out, either by requesting and taking up references from their bank, or by enquiring with a credit reference agency which can tell you if they have any County Court Judgements, bankruptcy orders, or poor credit history against them. The Late Payment Act allows you to charge interest on any overdue payments although in practice it is better to ensure that your customers are creditworthy at the outset, as no amount of interest can provide adequate recompense if the original debt remains unpaid.

You must monitor your debtors (people who owe you money) and creditors (people you owe money to) at all times. If one of your customers has not paid you in accordance with your agreed terms, do not put off taking action to ensure payment. Talk to your customer early about the non-payment to see if it is just an oversight or if there is a problem. Communication is vital in the collection of outstanding debtors, but if it gets to a stage where, despite promises, payment is still not forthcoming, consider stronger measures to recover the amount owing. Initially a letter from your solicitor might bring about the desired result; if not, then you may have to consider legal action for recovery of the money. However, this can be expensive and you should think long and hard before embarking on such a course. For this reason, you will be able to see the importance of dealing only with customers who you think will pay you promptly.

Profit

Profit is different to cashflow. As we have already seen, cashflow is actual cash received into, or paid out of, your business. Profit is only a paper measurement and not actual cash.

In Chapter 7 we looked at the Profit and Loss Account and the sort of items which appear in it. We saw that by deducting all of the expenditure of your business from the sales revenue, we were left with the net profit. This is not the same as the cashflow generated by your business, for a number of reasons:

- Sales revenue may include invoices for sales, for which you have not yet actually been paid
- Expenditure may include items which you have received invoices for, but which you have not yet actually paid
- Expenditure may include what are known as 'non-cash' items, such as depreciation (see Chapter 7). You don't actually write out a cheque to pay depreciation because it is a paper entry in the books of your business, not a cashflow item

What Is the Difference Between Cashflow and Profit?

Let's look at an example to help you understand the difference between cashflow and profit.

Assume you make a sale to the value of £1000. To make that sale you need to buy stock to the value of £500. Therefore, your profit is £500 (£1000 minus £500).

However, you only receive cash when your customer pays you, so until that time, you have actually not generated any cashflow for your business. In fact, if you have had to pay for the £500 of stock already then your cashflow is actually negative £500 until you receive payment from your customer.

You can see then, using the above example, that a profit of £500 can also be cashflow of negative £500. Both are correct but the example clearly illustrates the importance of understanding the difference between cashflow and profit, so that you can ensure that the cashflow of your business is always positive.

Why It Is Important to Understand the Difference Between Cashflow and Profit

Running out of cash is the prime reason why businesses fail. Often this is because the owner of the business has not given cashflow issues the time and attention they require. You need to constantly monitor cashflow and plan ahead to ensure that your business does not run out of cash to pay its bills.

I cannot stress this point strongly enough - it is absolutely vital that you understand the difference between cash and profit. Remember that profit does not pay bills, cash does!

10

Forecasting the Financial Performance of Your Business

In the preceding chapters we have looked at some accounting basics. Accounting forms the basis not only for reporting what has happened to your business in the past, by way of the profit and loss account and the balance sheet, but also for reporting what you expect to happen to your business in the future. This is called Forecasting.

Forecasting for a New Business

If you are just setting up your business, or are thinking of setting up a business, it is vital that you prepare some forecasts of how you expect your business to operate financially. This is sometimes called preparing a budget, which was covered in Chapter 2. Go back and have a look at that chapter now if you are unsure about how to prepare a budget. A specimen budget is also included as Appendix 2 of this book.

Forecasting Once Your Business Is Up and Running

Many business owners think that once their business is up and running they don't need to bother with forecasts any more. This is a big mistake and is a contributory factor in many business failures.

Even though your business may have been trading for some time, you still need to think about forecasting its performance into the future. This may be for a number of reasons, such as:

- A lot of your expenses are likely to rise each year, as suppliers increase their prices. This may include not only suppliers of stock, but also suppliers of electricity or telephone services. In addition your wage costs may increase because your workforce may expect an annual pay rise
- A new competitor may have opened up in your area and you will need to think about the impact this may have on your business if they start to take custom away from you and your sales start to fall
- You may be approaching a bank for an overdraft or loan. They will almost certainly want to see a forecast for your business, to help reassure them that you can afford to repay the overdraft or loan they are thinking of giving you
- All good business people plan ahead, often having at least 3 forecasts – a one year (called a short-term plan), a five year (called a medium-term plan) and a ten year (called a long-term plan). This enables them to set out where they want to take their business in the future and what they want to achieve. After all, if you don't plan something, how will you know when you achieve it? Successful business people will tell you that **if you fail to plan, then you plan to fail**. They recognise the importance of planning ahead. Preparing forecasts is an essential part of this process

- It is a good idea to plan for an increase in profit each year. A figure of between 10% and 15% would not be unreasonable. This will help you to keep focused on driving your business forward. It is worth reflecting that if your business is standing still – that is, the profit is the same each year – then in reality it is actually going backwards, because everyone else's business is moving forward. Therefore, you will get left behind unless you continually strive to grow the profit of your business each year

Forecasting Cashflow

Cashflow is the amount of money you need to keep your business running, and I make no apology for repeating at this stage a phrase which should be at the forefront of your mind at all times when you are running a business. It is '**Cash is King**'.

As already mentioned elsewhere in this book, the main reason businesses fail is lack of cash, as opposed to lack of profit. In Chapter 9 we looked at the difference between cash and profit, and if you are unsure what the difference is, then go back and have another look at Chapter 9 now, because it is absolutely vital that you understand this concept.

To work out how much cashflow you will need, you should prepare a cashflow forecast. We looked at how to do this in Chapter 3 under the heading 'Working Capital'.

Forecasting the Balance Sheet

If you are running a small business, it is unlikely that you will need to forecast the balance sheet of your business.

If you are approaching a bank or finance company for a loan they do not usually require you to produce a forecast balance sheet but merely a forecast profit and loss (or budget) for the business.

Forecasting a balance sheet is a complex task and if you are requested to provide one then you should speak to your accountant, who will be able to prepare it for you. Alternatively, accounting software packages such as those mentioned in Chapter 5 often contain forecasting programs, and these will include programs to help you forecast your balance sheet. Essentially what happens is that you put in the numbers for the forecast profit and loss account (or budget) and the program automatically calculates the balance sheet as well. The program often needs balance sheet figures from previous years to be able to do this because it calculates the forecast assumptions based on what has happened in the business in the past. However, as already mentioned, if you are running a small business it is not likely that you will need to forecast a balance sheet.

11

Some Key Ratios to Understand in Relation to Your Business

There are a number of accounting ratios which are very important to the business owner, both in the way you run the business and also when approaching lenders for business funding. Understanding these ratios will help you manage the financial aspects of your business better and also enable you to present your business in the best light when approaching a bank or finance company for a business loan or overdraft.

Gearing

We mentioned gearing in Chapter 8, but let's now look at this ratio in more detail because it is a key ratio to the financial health of your business.

Gearing indicates the amount of debt in a business relative to its assets. In other words, what proportion of assets is funded by debt of all forms (for example loans from the bank or family, and creditors). The generally accepted safety benchmark is to have a gearing ratio of no more than 65%. This means that debt is funding approximately two-thirds of the business and the owner the remaining one-third. There are a number of definitions of gearing but for our purposes we will adopt the formula:

Total Liabilities divided by Total Assets

If the resulting percentage is greater than 65% then your business is in danger of being 'over-borrowed'. This means that it has a very high level of debt to fund and this may put your business in a weak financial position, with more of the profit and cashflow having to be allocated to funding that debt. Ideally, therefore, the gearing ratio of your business should be no greater than 65%. A bank or finance company will view a business more favourably if its gearing ratio is 65% or less.

Liquidity

This is another key ratio or indicator of the financial well-being of your business and is thus worthy of further mention.

Liquidity indicates the amount of liquid assets available to fund short-term debt (for example bank overdrafts and creditors). By liquid assets we mean those assets which can be turned into cash relatively quickly, for example stock and debtors. The generally accepted safety benchmark is to have a liquidity ratio of at least 150%. The formula for liquidity is as follows:

Current Assets divided by Current Liabilities

Have a look now at the example balance sheet in Appendix 5. You can see that current assets are shown at 'A' and current liabilities are shown at 'D'. It is the totals of these two categories which are used in the formula for liquidity. Your aim should be to always have a minimum ratio of 150%. Put another way, this means that your current liabilities are covered 1.5 times by your current assets. This would indicate that you have more than sufficient liquid assets to turn into cash should you need to pay all of your current liabilities in a hurry. If your liquidity ratio is greater than 150% then a bank or finance company will view it more favourably. If your liquidity ratio is less than 100%, this means that your business has insufficient liquid assets to meet all its short-term, or immediate, liabilities. This is not a good situation to be in and would certainly be viewed as a key weakness by a bank or finance company.

Cashflow

This is a key indicator of the financial strength of your business, because it measures the amount of cash the business is generating. You will recall that cashflow is arguably the most important issue your business will have to deal with and the stronger the cashflow of your business, the stronger your overall business will be.

In a small business, cashflow is often calculated in the following way:

Net Profit (from the Profit and Loss Account) + Any non-cash items such as Depreciation shown in the Profit and Loss Account.

The result is the cashflow generated by the business. Obviously, the higher the figure the better because it means your business is generating more cashflow.

The resulting figure can then be compared with, for example, the value of loan repayments the business has to make. Clearly, it is better if the cashflow figure is well in excess of the amount of the repayments which have to be funded out of that cashflow. If the cashflow is less than the amount of any repayments then the business is not generating sufficient cash to meet its loan obligations, which is obviously not a good situation to be in. Let's look at an example to illustrate this point:

XYZ Limited – Profit and Loss figures for 12 months ending 31st March XXXX

Net Profit per the Profit and Loss Account	£ 50,000
Add back Depreciation and Amortisation	£ 2,500
Net Cashflow generated	£ 52,500
Loan Repayments £1,500 per month (x12)	£ 18,000
Net Surplus of cash after meeting loan repayments	£ 34,500

It can be seen from the above example that this business is in a good position, with more than sufficient cash generated to meet all its loan repayments.

Sales Growth

It is important to be able to measure the sales growth of your business from year to year for two reasons. Firstly, it will help you understand how your business is performing and whether it is growing or not. It is probably fair to say that as a minimum your business should grow in line with inflation. This is because the costs of running your business will probably escalate each year broadly in line with inflation so you need to ensure that your sales do likewise, otherwise you may find that the profit you are making reduces from year to year.

Secondly, a bank or finance company will like to see your business achieving a continuous, steady growth in sales from year to year. This will give them comfort that your business is growing and thus they will feel that it is more worthy of their support.

The formula for calculating sales growth is:

Increase in Sales Year 1 to Year 2, divided by Sales Year 1, multiplied by 100.

Let's look at an example to illustrate this point:

XYZ Limited

Sales in 2005	£ 100,000
Sales in 2006	£ 125,000
Increase	£ 25,000

Therefore, using the formula above, the calculation would be:

£25,000 divided by £100,000 multiplied by 100 = Sales Growth of 25%

Gross Profit Margin

This ratio is also sometimes called Gross Profit Percentage.

In Chapter 7 we talked about gross profit margin and how you can use it to help you monitor the progress of your business, and also to work out the breakeven amount of sales. You will recall that it is calculated as follows:

Gross Profit divided by Sales, multiplied by 100

This ratio is an important one when managing the financial position of your business because it enables you to see not only how your gross profit margin changes over time, and to make sure that it is not falling, but also how you can use the ratio to try to improve the profitability of your business. Let's look at an example to illustrate this point:

XYZ Limited	**2005**	**2006**
Sales	£ 100,000	£ 100,000
Gross Profit	£ 75,000	£ 80,000
Gross Profit Margin	75%	80%
Expenses	£ 50,000	£ 50,000
Net Profit	£ 25,000	£ 30,000

You can see from the above example that XYZ Limited improved its gross profit margin in 2006 to 80%, compared with a figure of 75% in 2005 Whilst being an increase of 5 percentage points it is actually an increase of 6.7% (£80,000 divided by £75,000 multiplied by 100).

Expenses stayed the same in 2006 so the net profit of the business grew to £30,000 from £25,000 due to the improved gross profit margin. This represents an increase of 20% when comparing the 2006 figure with the 2005 figure (£30,000 divided by £25,000 multiplied by 100).

You can see therefore that an increase of just **6.7%** in the gross profit margin has led to an increase of **20%** in net profit. This illustrates the power of achieving an improvement in the gross profit margin of your business. Even a relatively small increase in gross profit margin can have an exponential effect on net profit. You should therefore understand what the current gross profit margin of your business is, and seek ways to increase that margin because this can have a significant impact on your business's profitability.

Net Profit Margin

We have already touched on net profit in the example above. Net Profit Margin is calculated as follows:

Net Profit divided by Sales, multiplied by 100

Using the example in the previous section, the net profit margin in 2005 was 25% (£25,000 divided by £100,000 multiplied by 100) and in 2006 it was 30% (£30,000 divided by £100,000 multiplied by 100).

It is important to monitor the net profit margin to ensure that it is not falling. If you find that this is the case, you need to investigate and understand why it is falling and take corrective action. This is called managing the finances of your business –

understanding why something is happening and taking action as necessary.

If you approach a bank for a loan or overdraft for your business, they will look at your net profit margin, and will feel more comfortable if it is stable or growing. They will feel less comfortable if it is falling! Remember that the object of the game when approaching a bank or finance company for a business loan or overdraft is to make them feel as comfortable as possible in lending money to your business. They will want to feel comfortable that the business is making progress and that it can afford to repay the loan. The more comfortable they feel, the more likely you are to get the loan or overdraft.

Interest Cover

This is an important ratio if your business is considering, or already is, borrowing money from a bank or finance company. The ratio will help convince the bank that your business can afford to borrow money, and it is calculated as follows:

Net Profit plus Interest Expense, divided by Interest Expense

Interest expense is defined as the interest portion only, on loans and overdrafts. Let's look at an example to illustrate how to calculate the ratio and what it means in the context of your business borrowing money from a bank or finance company:

XYZ Limited

Sales	£ 100,000
Gross Profit	£ 80,000
Interest Expense	£ 5,000
Other Expenses	£ 45,000
Total Expenses	£ 50,000
Net Profit	£ 30,000

Interest Cover (see formula above) = £30,000 plus £5,000 (equals £35,000), divided by £5,000

Result = 7 times cover. This means that the business is covering its interest costs 7 times, which is a very strong performance. Generally a bank or finance company will be looking for a minimum of 1 to 1.5 times cover in order to feel comfortable. Obviously, the higher the level of cover, the more comfortable they will feel.

12

Monitoring the Financial Performance of Your Business

As you move forward in your business it is important to monitor its financial performance, so that you can take action if the results are not as expected. This is called 'managing the finances' of your business and is something that larger businesses do as a matter of course. If you are serious about making a success of your business then there are a series of key ratios which you should be monitoring on a regular basis, ideally monthly, to ensure that your business is moving in the right direction financially.

Accounting software packages can provide you with most, if not all, of the ratios we will now discuss. This makes accessing the information much less time consuming, assuming that your bookkeeping is up to date!

The key ratios to monitor are as follows:
Sales Growth
Gross Profit Margin
Net Profit Margin
Trade Debtor Days (also called Trade Receivables Days)
Trade Creditor Days (also called Trade Payables Days)
Stock Turnover Days

We looked at the first three ratios (Sales Growth, Gross Profit Margin and Net Profit Margin) in Chapter 11 so in this chapter we will concentrate on the remaining three – Trade Debtor Days, Trade Creditor Days and Stock Turnover Days.

Trade Debtor Days

Trade Debtors are amounts owed to your business by your customers for goods and services supplied by your business. Obviously if you trade on cash terms with your customers then you will not have any trade debtors, for example if you run a corner shop and people pay cash as they purchase items from you.

The formula for working out Trade Debtor Days is:

Trade Debtors Outstanding divided by Sales, multiplied by 365.

The above formula assumes you are using annual figures. If you are using monthly figures then the formula would be:

Trade Debtors Outstanding divided by monthly Sales, multiplied by 30, 31 or 28 (depending on which month you are looking at).

For example, if a business has annual sales of £150,000 and its trade debtors outstanding are £10,000 then its trade debtor days would be 24 (£10,000 divided by £150,000 multiplied by 365).

Remember that trade debtors is a balance sheet item and can be found in the 'Current Assets' section of the balance sheet. Sales are a profit and loss account item.

The importance of knowing what your trade debtor days are is that you can then compare this with what you know to be the credit terms you have negotiated with your customers. For example, if you have negotiated credit terms with your customers of 30 days and you calculate that your trade debtor days is 60, then this indicates that you are not getting paid by your customers in accordance with the terms you have agreed with them. This may be their fault in that, for example, they may not have the money with which to pay you. Alternatively, some of the blame may lie with you for not having a robust debtor control system, where you chase up your customers immediately the due payment day is past. Sometimes it can be a simple issue of the invoice being mislaid, in which case prompt chasing by you immediately the due payment date is past will often reveal if this is the reason for non-payment.

In all cases, if your trade debtor days are running higher than you expect, then you need to take action to bring them back under control. This may involve reviewing your current system for chasing up your debtors, to improve the efficiency of collection.

Trade Creditor Days

Trade Creditors are amounts owing to your suppliers for goods and services supplied to your business. Obviously if you trade on cash terms with your suppliers then you will not have any trade creditors.

The formula for working out Trade Creditor Days is:

Trade Creditors Outstanding divided by Cost of Goods Sold, multiplied by 365.

The above formula assumes you are using annual figures. If you are using monthly figures then the formula would be:

Trade Creditors Outstanding divided by monthly Cost of Goods Sold, multiplied by 30, 31 or 28 (depending on which month you are looking at).

For example, if a business has annual cost of goods sold of £50,000 and its trade creditors outstanding are £5,000 then its trade creditor days would be 36 (£5,000 divided by £50,000 multiplied by 365).

Remember that trade creditors is a balance sheet item and can be found in the 'Current Liabilities' section of the balance sheet.

Cost of goods sold is a profit and loss account item. You will recall that we looked at cost of goods sold in Chapter 7.

The importance of knowing what your trade creditor days are is that you can then compare this with what you know to be the credit terms you have negotiated with your suppliers. For example, if you have credit terms of 30 days and you calculate that your trade creditor days is 60, then this indicates that you are not paying your suppliers in accordance with the terms you have agreed with them. This may be caused by you not having a robust payment system within your business, such that invoices are received by you but then not diarised appropriately for payment on the due date.

It is very important to have good relationships with your trade creditors because there may come an unforseen time when you need to pay them slightly later than normal. If you have good relationships with them they are much more likely to agree to this than if you are always late paying them.

It is also worth noting that if you have the available cash you might consider approaching your trade creditors and asking them for a discount if you pay them earlier than the previously agreed terms. Often, suppliers will be very open to such approaches because it means they get their cash quicker, so it is worth asking the question, but only if you are sure you have the available cashflow.

Banks and finance companies will also look at your trade creditor days' ratio if you approach them for a business loan or overdraft. They will do this because it gives them an indication of cashflow pressure in a business. For example, if your trade creditor days are 90 and the normal period for your type of business is 30 then the bank or finance company will be wary that your business may be having cashflow problems, and not have enough cash to pay trade creditors on the due date.

Stock Turnover Days

This ratio measures the efficiency of a business in managing stock or inventory. As a general rule, lower stock turnover days indicates greater efficiency, and higher stock turnover days indicates less efficiency. It is sometimes helpful to think of stock as cash stacked on your shelves – the more stock you have the more cash you will have tied up – perhaps too much. Therefore this is a good ratio to monitor to ensure that you do not have more stock than you need to run your business effectively.

The formula for working out Stock Turnover Days is:

Stock divided by Cost of Goods Sold, multiplied by 365.

As with trade debtor days and trade creditor days, the above formula assumes you are using annual figures. If you are using monthly figures then the formula would be:

Stock divided by monthly Cost of Goods Sold, multiplied by 30, 31 or 28 (depending on which month you are looking at).

For example, if a business has annual cost of goods sold of £50,000 and its stock figure is £10,000 then its stock turnover days would be 73 (£10,000 divided by £50,000 multiplied by 365).

Remember that stock is a balance sheet item and can be found in the 'Current Assets' section of the balance sheet. You will recall that cost of goods sold is a profit and loss account item.

The importance of knowing what your stock turnover days are is that you can then compare the result with previous periods to see if the figure is increasing, decreasing, or remaining stable. If it is increasing then this may indicate that you have some stock which is not moving or is obsolete. Once you identify which stock this is you might consider having a sale to try to move it. After all, it is better to get something for it rather than just letting it sit on your shelves. This is one of the reasons why you will see stores having sales – they recognise that it is not good business practice to just leave stock on the shelves; it is better to try to convert it into cash by selling it, even if that means discounting the price.

Cash at Bank

Whilst not strictly a ratio, it would not be right to leave a chapter about the key things to monitor in your business without mentioning cash at bank.

I make no apology for repeating that cashflow is arguably the most important issue which you should be addressing when running your business, not only in the early days of your business but throughout its entire lifetime. Running out of cash is the prime reason why businesses fail, and often this is because the owner of the business has not given cashflow issues the time and attention they require.

Each month you should compare the figure in your accounts for 'cash at bank' with your actual bank statement, to ensure that they are the same. This is called reconciling the bank account and you will recall that we talked about bank reconciliation in more detail in Chapter 5. Go back and have a look at that chapter now if you are unsure about the reconciliation process, because it is a vital element in the success of your business and one which you need to be familiar with.

13

RUNNING A BUSINESS FROM HOME

Operating a business from home is in some ways very different from operating a business from an office, factory or shop. There are advantages and disadvantages to running a business from home, as well as accounting and taxation issues which you will need to be aware of. You will also need to consider local council planning issues and insurance for your business assets.

Advantages

One of the main reasons people choose to set up and run their own business is lifestyle.

Running a business from home is big attraction to a lot of people because it means they no longer have to travel to and from a separate place of work, with all the stress that commuting can bring such as over-crowded trains and buses, traffic jams and lack of convenience, especially if there is not a train or bus station near to your workplace, or if there is no car parking close by. If you are running your business from home you can almost fall out of bed and straight into work!

The fact that you no longer have to commute also means that you save all that wasted time each day. Over the years this can add up to a significant amount of time, which can perhaps be better utilised. For example, you may use the time saved each day to go for a walk, or go to the gym, thereby improving your health. I would strongly recommend this because you will also find that some form of exercise actually sets you up for the day ahead and energises you for the tasks you have to do. It also gives you some valuable thinking time in which to plan what you want to do with your business and how you are going to take it forward.

A significant advantage to running a business from home is that it keeps your costs down. In the early days of running your business it is vital to keep costs as low as possible, to maximise your chances of making a profit. Running your business from home will save on rent (which you would pay if you leased separate business premises), travelling expenses (because you will no longer be commuting to and from your place of work each day) and other costs such as business rates.

Running your business from home can also mean that you are more productive than you would be if you worked in an office with other people. The lack of distractions, such as passing the time of day with colleagues, means that you are able to concentrate on what you are doing and are thus more productive.

Another major advantage home businesses have over larger businesses is what we might call business flexibility. By this I mean that home businesses are often better placed to move quickly to take advantage of new technology and trends. This can give them a competitive advantage over larger businesses, which are often slower to adapt to such changes.

Finally, and this is one of the key reasons why many people start up a home business, running a business from home allows you greater flexibility to manage work and family responsibilities. A lot of people are seeking ways to spend more time with their families, particularly if they have young children, and running a business from home can help you better manage this issue. For example, if it fits in with your customers, you can take time out of work during the day to spend with family; then, once the children have gone to bed, you can settle down to some work. This is something which would not be very practicable if you worked in an office because you would have to leave the office, drive home to spend time with the family then drive back to the office after the children had gone to bed. Once you had finished your work for the day you would then have to drive home again! You can see that this would not be an efficient use of time and would also increase the costs of running your business through, for example, increased petrol or travel costs.

Disadvantages

One of the main disadvantages of running a business from home is the difficulty of separating work time from family time. For example, it can be very hard for children to understand why you cannot play with them if you are at home. They may not understand that you are trying to run a business, so make sure that everyone in your family understands how things will work and ensure that you have their full support before you start your business. Then ensure that you maintain the personal discipline you will need to see this through. It can be a great help if you have a defined, separate space within your home where you will operate from. In this way everyone will know that this space is your work space and that when you are in that space you need to be left alone to get on with running your business.

Another disadvantage people find when running a business from home is the lack of social contact. If you have been used to working in a large office or factory, with lots of people around you, it can be difficult to adapt to working either on your own or with a minimal number of people. Often people find that they don't have anyone to bounce ideas off, or just to pass the time of day with as a way of interacting socially with other people. This can lead to a sense of loneliness. Obviously you will still be interacting with your customers but this is different from interacting with friends and colleagues on a social level. If you are a really social person you may find that running a business on your own from home is not for you.

If you are thinking of running your business from home, make sure you consider fully the amount of space you will need in order to operate the business effectively. For example, if you will need to hold large amounts of stock, have you got sufficient space to keep it all in? Also, consider what sort of stock you will be holding. For example, is it is likely to be something which is potentially flammable? If you do not have sufficient space at home to store your stock, or the nature of the stock makes it not advisable to store it at home, then you should consider renting storage space instead. There are plenty of storage providers around so have a look in the telephone book to find your local ones. Often they will give you the choice of long-term or monthly agreements. This can be extremely helpful in providing you with flexibility, which is very important when you first set up your business. Your business needs to be able to operate efficiently, so make sure that you have sufficient space within your home to be able to do this, otherwise consider the option of renting storage space instead.

Another potential disadvantage, related to the issue of space, is what you will do if a customer wants to visit you. If you don't think that it will be appropriate to have them come to your home, then consider asking them if you can come to their place of work instead. Often, customers are pleased if you do this because it shows an interest in their business and also it saves them time and money travelling to you. A further alternative might be to use a serviced office. This is where a company rents out offices on a 'needs' basis. This can be very useful for holding meetings, particularly if you are bringing together a large number of people. You can find details of serviced office suppliers in Yellow Pages.

One significant disadvantage of working from home is the lack of support staff around you. You may have previously worked for a large organisation where there were additional people carrying out important support roles, such as secretarial, computer and IT, human resources, accounting and marketing support. These are all important, and just because you now run your own business it does not mean that you can ignore them. They are roles for which you will now have to take primary responsibility, and may even have to perform yourself, as well as running your business. For example, it might be that where you previously worked, if your computer or your printer broke down you would make a quick telephone call and someone would come running to fix it for you. When running your own business from home you will not have that level of support and you will need to think about what you will do if that eventuality occurs.

One way you can do this is to build a support team of external providers of these services. The starting point is to think about all of the above areas and put them into order of priority. For example, if you are intending to just run your business yourself initially, without any staff, then human resources support would be a low priority for you. Conversely, if you are running a business in which you are absolutely reliant on your computer working all the time, then finding external IT support would be a major priority. Have a look in the Yellow Pages and talk to suppliers to find out costs and, importantly, response times. If your IT support supplier will take a week to come and see you each time you have a problem, that will not be much help if you need your computer to enable your business to function. When comparing external suppliers, find out what their normal and emergency response time guarantees are, and if they provide support outside of normal office hours. Make sure that with all of your external suppliers they can meet your needs, and ensure that you have this in writing when you sign up with them so that there are no misunderstandings later on. Finally, ensure that you take into account the cost of these external suppliers when preparing the budget for your business (see Chapter 2 – Completing a Feasibility Study).

You can see from the above that there are numerous advantages and disadvantages to setting up and running your own business from home. The important thing is not to over-emphasise the advantages, nor to be put off by the disadvantages, but to weigh up both sides of the argument carefully before deciding whether running your business from home is a viable option for you. Your final decision will be influenced very much by your own personality and your personal goals; therefore, it may help you to jot down what you see as the personal 'pluses and minuses' of running your business from home,. If the pluses outweigh the minuses then you can be reassured that you are making the right decision for you.

Accounting and Taxation

As already mentioned, one of the main advantages of running a business from home is that you keep the costs of the business to a minimum. However, you must still keep accurate records of all costs and outgoings incurred in the running of your business, both for accounting and taxation purposes.

In order to be able to claim business expenses which you can offset against your business income for taxation purposes, HM Revenue & Customs requires you to be able to justify the proportion of expenses which relate solely to your business activities, as distinct from your private usage. For example, if you are claiming a proportion of your electricity bill as a business expense, you must be able to demonstrate that the proportion you are claiming is accurate. The best way to do this is to dedicate a part of your home solely for business use. This may take the form of a spare bedroom or a garage which you convert into an office. Measure the space taken up by the part of your home which is used for business purposes and claim expenses proportionately. For example, if your office takes up 10% of the total floor space of your home then a claim of 10% of your electricity bill (including VAT) would not be unreasonable. The same measurement can then be applied to other utility bills.

You may consider claiming a proportion of your mortgage interest as a business expense, using the proportion method outlined above. However, you must bear in mind that if you do this you will probably lose your prime residence capital gains tax allowance in the same proportion. What I mean is this – your place of residence is usually free of capital gains tax, so if you sell your home at a profit there is, generally, no capital gains tax on that profit. However, if you have been claiming a proportion of your mortgage interest as a business expense, at say 10%, then 10% of the profit you make on the sale of your house may be subject to capital gains tax. This is a complex matter which requires careful consideration together with the advice of a qualified accountant.

For more information on what you can and cannot claim, visit the HM Revenue & Customs website (address in the Useful Addresses section at the end of this book) or speak to your accountant.

Planning Permission

You may require local council permission to operate your business from your home. Planning schemes administered by local councils often impose limitations on the use of residential premises for business purposes. It is advisable to check with your local council as to the zoning of your property and whether or not you will need permission to run your business from your home.

Insurance

It is important to insure your business assets against loss, theft etc. However, your normal home insurance policy will probably not cover you for operating a business from your home. For example, it will certainly not cover you for the loss of any stock which you are storing at home. In the same way, your car insurance policy will probably not cover you for business-related use of your car.

It is important therefore to advise your insurance company of what you intend to do and get them to issue an official notification confirming that they have been advised. This official notification will usually take the form of a revised policy schedule or a policy endorsement. It is unlikely that a brand new policy will be required. In this way there can be no argument at a later date should you need to make a claim.

Consideration for your neighbours

If you plan to run your business from home, have consideration for your neighbours and think how your business may affect them. For example, it may be that your customers will be visiting you at home and this may lead to an increase in traffic and potential parking problems, so think about that and how it might impact on your neighbours.

Also, if you intend to run a business which will produce noise or dust (for example you may be a cabinet maker or welder and plan to operate from your garage), think about how that might affect your neighbours. Not only is it the right thing to do, but it will also forestall potential problems for your business if a dispute arises with your neighbours in the future.

14

EARLY DAYS

You have now embarked on the journey of running your own business. The business is established and you are trading. It is very easy in these early days to become side-tracked by the day-to-day issues that arise, but it is important not to lose sight of your planned goals and strategy.

Research shows that many small business owners are under severe time pressures, working on average 63 hours a week. As a result of this, some of the more important 'management' areas tend to get neglected. Beware! Neglecting the important management issues is a recipe for disaster. It is vital to strike a balance between the day-to-day operation of your business and the long-term management of that business.

Cashflow

I have talked about the importance of cashflow on a number of occasions in this book, but I make no apology for labouring the point. Cashflow is arguably the most important issue which you should be addressing, not only in the early days of your business but throughout its entire lifetime. **Running out of cash is the prime reason why businesses fail.**

Customer Service

This is an area which a lot of businesses neglect – to their cost! It is absolutely vital to stay in touch with your customers, listening to what they are telling you about your products or services, how you deliver those products or services to them and how they feel about doing business with you. Each of your customers needs to feel that they are the most important customer to you – because in their eyes they are! Customers will often be prepared to pay a little more for good service; and if you serve them well, they will be more prepared to forgive you for any mistakes. These are both vital factors in the success of your business.

Always remember that people's buying decisions are based on emotions. Some people will try to argue that they are entirely objective when they buy something: researching the product or service, checking out its features and comparing the cost to similar products or services. Whilst it is true that they may do some or all of these things, ultimately they buy the product or service because of their emotional reaction to it. This may take the form of a good feeling about something (as in the case of a house), how fast it will go (in the case of a car), how well they look in it (in the case of a dress or suit).The deciding factor in taking the step to purchase a product or service may simply be that the whole buying experience is a good one. This may include making the whole process easy for the customer to complete and certainly includes making the customer feel valued. Remember – a happy customer will come back and buy from you again and again. Not only that, they will tell their friends about their experience, and this is the best form of advertising you can have.

An important part of the customer service 'experience' is that when you deliver your product or service, you get it right first time, every time. First impressions count and you do not get a second chance to make a good first impression. This may include the layout of your store (if you have one), your appearance and professionalism when meeting a new customer for the first time, the appearance and courteousness of your staff, or even how you or your staff answer the telephone. A little tip here – whenever either you or your staff are answering the telephone try to ensure that you are smiling. It might sound a little silly but this 'feeling' will transmit down the line and your customer will pick up on it, even if subliminally, and will react positively. Conversely, if you or your staff are miserable this too will be picked up by the customer on the other end of the line, and this will damage your customer service.

Another useful tip is to always put yourself in the shoes of your customer. Imagine that you are them and think about how you would want to be treated if you were purchasing something from your business. Also think about how you would expect yourself to appear, from your customer's perspective, in the context of the type of business you are in. For example, if you are running a secretarial business it would be reasonable to assume that your customers would expect to see someone smartly dressed and businesslike in appearance. Turning up in a tracksuit and training shoes would not be appropriate and will not endear you to your customers!

Never be afraid to ask your customers what they think of your business and how they rate the service they receive from you. Customer feedback is arguably the most important piece of information you can receive. It will tell you what your customers like about doing business with you, and what they dislike, providing you with the opportunity to improve where necessary. The feedback may even highlight areas where you had no idea there was a problem!

Let it be your aim to provide your customers with 'world-class service'. Strive to be the very best at delivering your product or service to your customers. Have reward schemes for your staff to recognise outstanding customer service.This will be money well spent. It is worth repeating this fact – a happy customer will buy from you time and time again, and will be a great source of advertising for your business.

Get off the Dance Floor and on to the Balcony

It is absolutely vital that you do not become so immersed in the day-to-day running of your business that you lose sight of your strategy and goals. It is so easy in the early days to be chasing sales and attempting to find new customers, or to become overly involved in the production side of your business, that you lose sight of the direction for your business or do not give appropriate attention to the other important management areas, such as finance, cashflow and legal issues. For these reasons you need to set aside time to 'get off the dance floor', which is the day-to-day running of your business, and 'up on the balcony', which is the overview and strategic part of owning and running a business.

It is a good idea to allow yourself some time each day to 'get up on the balcony'. This might take the form of going for a walk or a swim for perhaps 30 minutes a day. Not only will this be good for your personal health, it will also be good for the health of your business. Leave your mobile telephone at home and spend that time thinking about where you are with your business, where you want to be and how you are going to get there. You might also use the time to think through any issues affecting your business. These could be internal issues such as production, employees or premises, or external issues such as legal problems, economic issues or competitor activity. It is amazing how productive and beneficial this time can be to your business. Your mind is clear and able to focus on important issues, rather than being overwhelmed by the day to day demands which your business places on you.

Monitoring Performance

We talked in Chapter 12 about some key ratios to monitor in your business, but it is worth repeating the importance of monitoring the performance of your business. This is an area where a lot of businesses fall short, but which is vital in helping you understand how your business is performing.

Think back to all that time you spent preparing a business plan, budget, and cashflow forecast. So often businesses then fail to monitor their actual performance against those forecasts, with the result that they fail to achieve their full potential or, even worse, the business fails completely. There is no point in setting out plans for your business and then not measuring your success (or otherwise) against those plans. The monitoring of actual performance against forecast performance enables you to take control of your business and to be an active manager of your business and its performance. It also enables you to foresee potential problems and thus take corrective action as appropriate.

By way of illustration of this point, let us consider the following scenario. You originally planned that your business would generate sales of £50,000 per month or £600,000 per annum. Yet after 3 months of trading you have only generated sales of £100,000. You will see that this indicates you are £50,000 behind your forecast for the 3 month period which, if continued unchecked, will equate to annual sales of £400,000, some £200,000 less than your forecast. It is vitally important that you understand why this has happened and take corrective action as early as possible. It will be no good waiting until the year has ended and then finding that your sales are £200,000 less than your forecast. By monitoring the position constantly you will learn much earlier that there is a problem and have the opportunity to do something about it promptly. In this example it may be that you have an order in hand which will bring your sales back in line with your forecast, or it may be that you have to reassess your marketing strategy to attract more customers. Whatever the reason, you will at least be aware of it at an earlier stage and be able to take appropriate action.

A vital element in monitoring performance is the regular reconciliation of your bank account, as mentioned in Chapter 5. You should regularly reconcile your business expenses and sales receipts with money in and out of your bank account. This will ensure that you have a good idea of how the cashflow of your business is performing and will help you identify money which has not yet been received or paid, thus helping you to avoid cashflow problems.

Another key element in monitoring the performance of your business is to know who your most profitable customers are and which of your products are the most profitable. Computerised bookkeeping software can help you do this (we looked at such software in more detail in Chapter 5). Clearly, if you can identify your most profitable customers and your most profitable products, you can focus your energies in these particular areas. Conversely, if you have unprofitable customers or products you can either take action to make them profitable or gradually exclude them.

The Emotional Rollercoaster

In the early days of your business, and indeed throughout its life, you will encounter what can be referred to as an 'emotional rollercoaster'.

By this I mean that there will be times of personal stress – doubts about whether you did the right thing in setting up your business and times when you feel like giving the whole thing up. There will be times when you are worried by the fact that you don't have enough sales, and there will be times when you are worried because you have too many sales and are wondering how you are going to meet all your delivery deadlines! These are the 'dips' on the emotional rollercoaster.

There will also be times of great personal satisfaction. Winning that big order you have been after for so long; making enough profit to expand your business or move to better premises; receiving a letter or word of appreciation from one of your customers; or winning an award for being a successful small business. These are the 'highs' on the emotional rollercoaster.

Do not be too concerned by these 'dips' and 'highs'. These emotions are common to all owners of businesses and therefore you are not the first to encounter them. Take heart from this. If you are aware that you will have some difficult times as well as some great times, you will be much more prepared for them, and thus be in a better position to deal with them when they occur.

Building a Support Team Around You

As your business grows and moves forward, start to build a team of advisors around you who can help and support you. This team can include people such as an accountant, a solicitor, a bank manager, a business coach/mentor and even fellow business people.

An accountant can help you prepare your financial year end accounts and advise on taxation/VAT issues, which are often very complex. The bookkeeping records which you will have kept, as outlined in Chapter 5 of this book, will help your accountant tremendously and thus reduce the amount of time he or she needs to spend on compiling your accounts. This not only saves you money in accountancy fees but also gives more time for you and your accountant to discuss taxation and business strategies.

An accountant can also help you with company law (if you are trading as a company) with regard to the completion of annual accounts, filing of appropriate returns to Companies House and generally complying with the various Companies Acts. He or she can also help you establish the company, ensuring that all the appropriate procedures and documentation are attended to.

A solicitor can help you in many ways, depending on the individual circumstances of your business. He or she can help you with partnership law if you are thinking of trading as a partnership. This can include advice on the legal position of partners and help in drawing up a partnership agreement, which is essential if you intend to trade as a partnership (see Chapter 4). He or she can also help you with property law if you are going to operate your business from premises other than your own home. This can include scrutiny of any property lease agreements you may be thinking of entering into.

Your solicitor can also assist you by checking any contracts you may be thinking of signing with potential purchasers, suppliers or other parties. If you plan to purchase a franchise it is essential that your solicitor goes through the franchise agreement with you and checks it out for any onerous clauses or things you are agreeing to in the agreement which you weren't aware you had agreed to in negotiations with the franchisor.

Hopefully you will never become embroiled in litigation at any stage of your business; but if you do, the help and guidance of a solicitor will be absolutely vital because the issues and procedures can be extremely complex, and the costs of getting it wrong can be huge. If you see potential problems ahead, get your solicitor involved as early as possible. This will minimise the risk that the matter becomes too far advanced before you try to do something about it. Don't do as the ostrich did and bury your head in the sand!

A solicitor can also help you with employment law. In recent years employment law has become very complex and unless proper procedures are followed at all times, the financial penalties can be very large. The same rule applies to Health and Safety laws, which are becoming ever more complex and potentially costly to the person running their own business. The Government also provides advice on these matters and further information can be found on the websites listed in Appendix 6 to this book.

Building a working relationship with your bank manager can be vital. This will maximise the chances of the bank supporting your business financially. It may be that your business needs some short-term help paying expenses, pending you receiving monies owing to the business by your customers, or it may be that you want to expand the business or purchase new premises. To achieve all of these things you will need the support of your bank manager. If he or she has seen your business plan, and is kept informed of how the business is progressing, you are much more likely to receive the help and support of the bank. Being able to provide him or her with up-to-date records of how the business is performing financially will also greatly assist in this process (see Chapter 5).

Having a business coach or mentor can be very helpful, particularly in the early days of your new business. Setting up and running your own business can be a very lonely experience at times and having someone who you can talk to about your business and the challenges facing it can be extremely helpful. You can talk to your coach or mentor about how the business is progressing, problems it is facing and even use them as a sounding board for any ideas you have for improving the way you are doing things. Your coach or mentor might be your accountant or solicitor, but a specialist business coach gives you a further person to help you, and one who is experienced in helping businesses just like yours to grow and succeed. In the UK we are fortunate to have organisations such as BusinessLink and Enterprise Agencies, which are Government-funded organisations providing support, advice and information on all aspects of setting up and running a business. They have advisers who can help you with a multitude of issues you may face, such as how to start exporting or dealing with Information Technology. Details of how to get in touch with these organisations can be found in Appendix 6 of this book.

Fellow business people can also be valuable, as people with whom you can talk about and share the day-to-day issues and problems you face in running your business. In all likelihood they have already experienced the same problems you are facing and can provide valuable advice and support. In addition, fellow business people may become future customers of yours once they know what it is you are selling, so meeting with such people can grow your sales as well as providing help and support. There are a number of forums where business people can get together, relax a bit, and discuss issues and problems they are facing in their businesses. These include Chambers of Commerce, Rotary Clubs and Small Business Networking Clubs. You can usually find details of these organisations in your local press, telephone book or via the internet.

Running your own business can potentially expose you to very complex legal and operational issues. Seeking appropriate advice will ensure that your business is better protected, legally and financially, at all times. The support and guidance of a good adviser will ensure that you minimise the potential pitfalls and avoid them wherever possible. Thus, building a support team of advisors around you will ensure that your business continues to be successful.

A Final Word

I said in the introduction to this book that setting up and running your own business is a journey which can bring great personal satisfaction, independence, the ability to manage the business around your lifestyle and, hopefully, financial reward. I have also said that there will undoubtedly be times of difficulty and stress.

However, remain focused on the positive reasons why you embarked on the journey in the first place and, with a careful eye on the potential pitfalls, there is no reason why your business should not be a great success. I hope that this book will help you in your journey.

Glossary

Accounting
A system which measures business activities, processes that information into reports and financial statements, and communicates the findings to decision makers.

Accounting Software
Computer software packages which can help you complete the essential records you need to keep for your business. Also referred to as bookkeeping software.

Assets
Items which are owned by a business (such as motor vehicles) or are owing to that business (such as money owed to it by its customers).

Balance Sheet
A 'snapshot' of the assets and liabilities of a business at a given point in time.

Breakeven
The minimum level of sales needed to cover all expenditure of a business.

Budget
A forward-looking financial plan for your business, setting out the expected sales income, the costs of running the business, and the profit you hope to achieve.

Business Coach/Mentor

A person who can help you make your business more successful, by sharing their business experience and skills with you. A useful sounding board for any ideas you have for your business.

Business Plan

A written framework to help crystallise some of the issues most vital to the success of your business. It is absolutely essential to the success of your business.

Cash Book

A book used to record all the payments and receipts for a business; that is, all the money going in and out of that business.

Cashflow

Actual cash into and out of your business.Probably the most important issue you need to consider when running a business. Not to be confused with profit, which is only a paper entry.

Cashflow Forecast

A report showing the estimated cashflow of a business, based on its future plans.

Cost of Goods Sold

The direct costs of producing something for resale. Formula: Opening Stock plus Purchases of Stock, minus Closing Stock.

Creditors

People to whom a business owes money, such as suppliers. Sometimes called 'Payables'.

Credit Terms

The number of days you allow your customers before they have to pay you, and which your suppliers allow you before you have to pay them.

Current Asset

Generally an asset which can be turned into cash within a period of 12 months. Will include items such as debtors or stock.

Debtors
Money owed to a business by its customers. Sometimes called 'Receivables'.

Demographics
Statistics about people – for example, where they live and what age group they are in. Very useful when planning for your business, as demographics can tell you where your potential customers are located and who they might be, so that you can target your marketing more effectively.

Depreciating Asset
An asset which has a limited effective life and can be reasonably expected to decline in value over the period in which it is used.

Differentiation Strategy
How you make your product or service different to that offered by your competitors, so that customers will purchase from you rather than from them.

Direct Mail
A form of advertising, where you obtain a list of potential customers and send them details of your product or service either in the post or by dropping the details in their letter boxes. Also known (to its recipients) as 'Junk Mail'.

Double-Entry Bookkeeping
A system which accounts for every aspect of a transaction – where it came from and where it went to. This 'from' and 'to' aspect of a transaction is referred to by the term 'double-entry'.

Establishment Capital
The amount of money you will need just to set up your business, including the cost of items such as machinery, equipment, stationery, accounting software and initial stock.

Fixed Assets
Assets that are owned by a business for long-term use in that business, and not intended for resale. Examples are items such as buildings, machinery, motor vehicles and office equipment.

Fixed Asset Register
A register which records details of the fixed assets of a business

Gross Profit
Sales less Cost of Goods Sold (see above for definition of Cost of Goods Sold)

Gross Profit Percentage or **Gross Profit Margin**
Gross Profit divided by Sales, multiplied by 100. This should be monitored regularly to ensure that the percentage is stable or improving. If it is falling, corrective action may be required.

Information Technology
Computer equipment used to help you gather, store, use and exchange information.

Intermediaries
Persons acting between different parties. In a business context this refers to someone who sells your product or service for you, rather than you selling direct to the customer.

Invoice
A document issued by a business for the sale of goods (a Sales Invoice), or received by a business for goods bought (a Purchase Invoice).

Liabilities
Items which a business owes to others. Liabilities may include monies owing to suppliers (called Creditors), monies owing to the owner(s) of a business (called Shareholders Equity or Shareholders Funds), or loans owing to other parties (such as bank overdrafts and loans, and hire purchase loans).

Limited Company
A structure for the running of a business. The company is a separate legal entity from the owners/directors. Therefore, the owners/directors are not liable personally for the debts of the company (other than in certain exceptional circumstances, such as continuing to trade while knowing that the business is insolvent and unable to pay all of its debts).

Marketing Mix
The various marketing aspects of your business and how you can best employ them to make your business more successful.

Market Research
Research carried out to establish whether there is a market for your product or service.

Networking
Meeting with other business people to share knowledge and experiences. These people will also, hopefully, become new customers for your business or be able to recommend your business to people they know.

Non-Current Asset
An asset which is more long-term in nature, that is, it is likely to be part of the business for a period exceeding 12 months. Examples include motor vehicles, plant and machinery, or office equipment, which are likely to have a lifespan of more than 12 months.

Outsourcing
Having someone who is not an employee of your business carry out tasks for you. For example, having a bookkeeper do your bookkeeping for you rather than doing it yourself.

Overheads
The general costs involved in running a business. For example, wages, insurance, telephone, heat, light and power.

Partnership
A number of individuals who get together to run a business. Each individual is usually jointly and severally liable for the entire debts of the business.

Profit and Loss Account
An account which documents sales revenue (sometimes called turnover) and all expenditure associated with earning that revenue for the period specified (usually annually).

Purchases Ledger
A record of all the goods and services purchased by a business. Sometimes called the 'Creditors Ledger'.

Receivables
Money owed to a business by its customers. Sometimes called 'Debtors'.

Reconciliation
The process by which a business adds up all the cash into and out of the business (usually monthly) and checks this against its bank statement to ensure that the two agree.

Sales Ledger
A record of all the sales a business has made to its customers. Sometimes also called the 'Debtors Ledger'.

Sole trader
An individual who sets up their own business in their own name, or using a trading name. They are wholly responsible for the debts of the business.

SMART goals
Targets you set for your business which are **S**imple, **M**easurable, **A**chievable, **R**ealistic and **T**imely.

Stock
Goods manufactured or bought for resale by a business. Raw materials used to produce goods for resale may also be classified as stock.

Stocktake
A process whereby a business counts up all its stock and values it according to one of a number of methods. Usually carried out at the end of the financial year of that business, e.g. 31st March.

Strategic Management
The process by which a business owner considers, chooses and implements the strategies necessary to move their business forward.

SWOT analysis

An analysis of your business, where you consider the **S**trengths and **W**eaknesses of the business, and the **O**pportunities and **T**hreats with which the business is faced. Strengths and Weaknesses usually refer to **internal** issues of a business (staffing, premises, customer base etc). Opportunities and Threats usually refer to **external** issues (competitor activity, economic and legal issues etc).

Trading Stock

Anything produced, manufactured, acquired or purchased for manufacture, sale or exchange.

Web-Hosting Service

A company which will register, host and maintain your business website.

Working Capital

The amount of money you will need in order to keep your business running from day to day.

Appendix 1

BUSINESS PLAN CHECKLIST

Market

- What is your product or service?
- Who and where is your target market?
- Who is your competition? What do they charge for their product or service?
- What is your competitive advantage? What makes your product or service different from the competition? What will make it sufficiently different for customers to use your product or service rather than that of the competition?
- Advertising and Promotion – how will you get the message out to your target market that you have something they will want?
- Distribution Network – how will you deliver your product or service to your customers? Will you do it face to face; over the internet; or through a network of suppliers?

Objectives

- What is your vision for your business?
- What are the motivations which drive you to set up your business?

- Set yourself 'SMART' goals – **S**pecific, **M**easurable, **A**chievable, **R**ealistic, **T**imely
- What is your exit strategy? Do you intend to pass the business on to children in due course; or do you intend to sell the business when you retire; or do you intend to float the business on the Stock Market?

Resources

- What will be your business structure – sole trader, partnership, company?
- What human resources will you need? Will you need to employ staff to help you deliver your product or service?
- What physical resources will you need? Will you operate from home or will you need premises? What equipment will you need to enable you to operate effectively?
- What financial resources do you have? Have you got capital or cash which you can use to get the business going or will you need to borrow money to get started? Are you able to raise finance if required?

Finance

- How have you calculated your pricing? How does it compare with your competitors?
- What will be your profitability? How much profit will you make on each sale?
- What is your breakeven? How much profit do you need to make to cover all your overheads?
- Prepare some financial projections, particularly a cashflow forecast. Remember to allow for credit given/taken.
- Remember to monitor your finances, especially cashflow.

Ability

- What experience do you have in the line of business you are establishing?
- How committed are you to this venture?

SWOT analysis of your business

- **S**trengths
- **W**eaknesses
- **O**pportunities
- **T**hreats
- Strengths and Weaknesses usually refer to **internal** issues of a business (staffing, premises, customer base etc)
- Opportunities and Threats usually refer to **external** issues of a business (competitor activity, economic issues, legal issues etc).

Appendix 2

EXAMPLE BUDGET

Income	
Sales (A)	
Cost of Goods Sold (B)*	
Gross Profit (A - B = C)	
Expenses	
Accountancy Fees	
Advertising	
Bank Charges	
Cleaning	
Computer Costs	
Electricity	
General Expenses	
Hire of Equipment	
Insurances	
Legal Expenses	
Motor Vehicle Expenses	
Payroll Tax	
Pension Contributions	
Printing, Stationery & Postage	
Rent	
Repairs & Maintenance	
Salaries & Wages	
Telephone	
Travel	
Total Expenses (D)	
Net Profit (C - D)	

* Opening Stock, plus Purchases, minus Closing Stock

Appendix 3

EXAMPLE CASHFLOW FORECAST

	Jan	Feb	Mar	Apr	May	Jun	Jul	Aug	Sep	Oct	Nov	Dec	Totals
Income (A)													
Sales Collections													
Payments													
Creditor Payments (stock etc)													
VAT Payable													
Accountancy													
Advertising													
Bank Charges													
Cleaning													
General Expenses													
Insurances													
Light, Heat & Power													
Motor Expenses													
PAYE													
Pension Contributions													
Postage/Stationery													
Rent													
Repairs & Maintenance													
Salaries & Wages													
Staff Expenses													
Telephone													
Travel Expenses													
HP/Lease Payments													
Loan Payments													
Total Payments (B)													
Net Income/Payments (A-B=C)													
Opening Bank Balance (D)													
Closing Bank Balance (D+C)													

Appendix 4

EXAMPLE PROFIT AND LOSS ACCOUNT

Sales (A)	
Cost of Goods Sold (B)*	
Gross Profit (A - B = C)	
Expenses	
Accountancy Fees	
Advertising	
Bank Charges	
Cleaning	
Computer Costs	
Depreciation	
Electricity	
General Expenses	
Hire of Equipment	
Insurances	
Interest Paid	
Legal Expenses	
Motor Vehicle Expenses	
Pension Contributions	
Printing, Stationery & Postage	
Rent	
Repairs & Maintenance	
Salaries & Wages	
Telephone	
Travel	
Total Expenses (D)	
Net Profit (C - D)	

* Opening Stock, plus Purchases, minus Closing Stock

Appendix 5

EXAMPLE BALANCE SHEET

Current Assets (A)	
Cash	
Debtors	
Stock	
Non Current Assets (B)	
Property	
Plant & Machinery	
Motor Vehicles	
Office Equipment	
Total Assets (A + B = C)	
Current Liabilities (D)	
Creditors	
Bank Overdraft	
Non Current Liabilities (E)	
Long-Term Loans	
Total Liabilities (D + E = F)	
Net Assets (C – F = G)	
Owner's Equity (should be the same figure as 'G' above)	

Appendix 6

USEFUL ADDRESSES

Government Agencies

www.businesslink.gov.uk – BusinessLink. Advice and support on all aspects of setting up and running a business, grants, health and safety, sales and marketing, exporting, Information Technology

www.companieshouse.gov.uk – Companies House. Registering a company name, guidelines on filing annual accounts of companies

www.disclosure.gov.uk – Criminal Records Bureau. Criminal records checks for potential employees in sensitive positions.

www.dti.gov.uk – Department of Trade and Industry. Advice and information for businesses

www.hse.gov.uk – Health and Safety Executive. Advice and guidance on health and safety regulations for businesses

www.hmrc.gov.uk – HM Revenue & Customs. Taxation, National Insurance, VAT, starting a business, employing staff

www.ico.gov.uk – Information Commissioner's Office. Information on the Data Protection Act and the requirements you will need to adhere to

www.oft.gov.uk – Office of Fair Trading. Guidelines and rules covering business advertising

www.thepensionservice.gov.uk – The Pension Service. Guidance on pensions for the self-employed

www.sbs.gov.uk – Government-backed Small Business Service. Latest news for Small Businesses, research and statistics, links to other Government organisations and support

www.statistics.gov.uk – Office for National Statistics. Useful statistics on population demographics to assist with market research

Professional and Business Organisations

www.thebfa.org – British Franchise Association. Help and advice on franchising.

www.icaew.co.uk – Institute of Chartered Accountants in England and Wales. Help in finding an accountant for your business

www.lawsociety.org.uk – The Law Society. Help in finding a solicitor for your business

www.nfea.com – National Federation of Enterprise Agencies. Advice and information on setting up and running a business

www.princes-trust.org.uk – The Prince's Trust. Loans and grants for young people to set up a business

www.smallbiz.uk.com – Advice on numerous aspects of running a small business

www.wbda.co.uk – Women's Business Development Agency. Advice and support for women in business. Provides female business advisors to assist women setting up and running a small business